Laird Addis
Nietzsche's Ontology

To my grandchildren,

Hazen, Luken, Zoe

Laird Addis

Nietzsche's Ontology

ontos
verlag

Frankfurt I Paris I Lancaster I New Brunswick

Bibliographic information published by Deutsche Nationalbibliothek
The Deutsche Nastionalbibliothek lists this publication in the Deutsche Nationalbibliographie;
detailed bibliographic data is available in the Internet at http://dnb.ddb.de

North and South America by
Transaction Books
Rutgers University
Piscataway, NJ 08854-8042
trans@transactionpub.com

United Kingdom, Ire, Iceland, Turkey, Malta, Portugal by
Gazelle Books Services Limited
White Cross Mills
Hightown
LANCASTER, LA1 4XS
sales@gazellebooks.co.uk

Livraison pour la France et la Belgique:
Librairie Philosophique J.Vrin
6, place de la Sorbonne ; F-75005 PARIS
Tel. +33 (0)1 43 54 03 47 ; Fax +33 (0)1 43 54 48 18
www.vrin.fr

©2012 ontos verlag
P.O. Box 15 41, D-63133 Heusenstamm
www.ontosverlag.com

ISBN 978-3-86838-165-8

2012

No part of this book may be reproduced, stored in retrieval systems or transmitted
in any form or by any means, electronic, mechanical, photocopying, microfilming, recording or otherwise
without written permission from the Publisher, with the exception of any material supplied specifically for the
purpose of being entered and executed on a computer system, for exclusive use of the purchaser of the work.

Printed on acid-free paper
ISO-Norm 970-6
FSC-certified (Forest Stewardship Council)
This hardcover binding meets the International Library standard

Printed in Germany
by CPI buch bücher.de

NIETZSCHE'S ONTOLOGY

Table of Contents

Nietzsche's Texts

I	Introduction	1
II	Truth and Objectivity	7
III	Constant Change	24
IV	Substances and Things	41
V	Minds	71
VI	Causation	101
VII	Will to Power	119
	Bibliography	135
	Name Index	139
	Subject Index	141

INTRODUCTION

This is an essay about Nietzsche's ontology. Because ontology is a part of metaphysics and because, so it is sometimes said, Nietzsche is against metaphysics, one would assume that he would also be against ontology. Indeed, as for metaphysics, in a passage of 1888 in *The Twilight of the Idols* that could almost have been written by a hardcore logical positivist forty years later, he remarks:

> Today we possess science precisely to the extent to which we have decided to *accept* the testimony of the senses—to the extent to which we sharpen them further, arm them, and have learned to think them through. The rest is miscarriage and not-yet-science—in other words, metaphysics, theology, psychology, epistemology—or formal science, a doctrine of signs, such as logic and that applied logic which is called mathematics. In them reality is not encountered at all, not even as a problem—no more than the question of the value of such a sign-convention as logic. (TI "'Reason' in Philosophy" 3, Nietzsche's emphasis)

Like the logical positivists (and our contemporary New Agers who, to the distress of philosophers, have their own, related use of the term), Nietzsche usually regards metaphysics as being about, or putatively about, some kind of reality beyond our everyday world. So in being against metaphysics in this sense, he is affirming his deeply held conviction that the everyday world exhausts reality; there is no "other" world, of any kind. But he sometimes also uses the term as most contemporary philosophers do–as a kind of catch-all notion for any kind of investigation–conceptual, ontological, linguistic–into any aspect of reality, making the term virtually the same in meaning as 'philosophy' itself. *Pace* our contemporary conceptual analysts, there is no point in arguing about the real meanings of words, for there are no real meanings of words apart from the meanings people give them; and up-to-date dictionaries are the best guide as to what those are. But we may say that Nietzsche, whatever he says here or there about metaphysics, certainly propounds an ontology. And while it is not, by the usual measures, an ontology of the depth one finds in Aristotle or Leibniz or Brentano or Bergmann, it nevertheless addresses some of the basic questions.

The Cambridge Dictionary of Philosophy, curiously, has no entry on 'ontology' and refers the reader to the entry on 'metaphysics' where we read that ontology is the study of being itself or else the same as metaphysics (Audi, 1999, 564). A precise, though not necessarily historically well-grounded, notion of ontology comes from the person who, more than any other, brought the idea into, or back into, analytic philosophy; namely, Gustav Bergmann. Ontology, as he conceives it, asks what exists in the sense of what are the categories of the "simples" that make up reality (1959b, 54). For Bergmann, as for Nietzsche, the reality to be dealt with is the only reality there is or that we have any good reason to believe in–the everyday world of common experience as further understood by empirical science. Broadly put, it is a world of physical bodies in space and time, a few of which bodies "have" minds, and that are bound in their behavior by the laws of nature. Thus, in this sense, ontology does not concern itself with putative supernatural or otherworldly things, but is only a certain kind of understanding of this, our common, everyday world. And at least some of this form of understanding is *analytic* insofar as it is concerned with "simples". But it is not physics or chemistry, which have their own, different kind of analytic understanding of physical reality.

Still, what I am calling Nietzsche's ontology does not quite correspond to this, or any, formal definition of 'ontology', although the notion of analysis to simples plays some role. I submit that we can get at a comprehensive understanding of his basic philosophical theory of the nature of reality by considering his views on five major categories of that reality: constant change, physical objects, minds, causation, and will to power. Perhaps what is most importantly absent from such a list is space and time; but, while I will have occasion to mention them, the fact is that Nietzsche had almost nothing of philosophical interest to say about them. For the most part, this lack is of no importance to anything else that he did say nor, therefore, to anything I have to say about his ontology.

Two of these categories–constant change and will to power–are peculiar to Nietzsche, especially the latter, while the other three–physical objects, minds, and causation–are categories that any comprehensive ontology would include. But I think that Nietzsche would agree that, in an important sense, "all there is" are bodies, a tiny percentage of which "have" minds, which exist in space and time and are subject to laws of nature. Constant change and will to power are not separate realms of entities, so to speak, but instead what Nietzsche believes to be features of bodies and minds. Still, treating them separately will, if I am not mistaken, give us a clearer understanding of what I am calling Nietzsche's ontology.

* * *

I am very much inclined to the view that, in an important sense, there are two Nietzsches. One is the sober naturalist–the believer in the value and the pre-eminence of the empirical sciences and of logic and mathematics (as the quote above suggests), the denier of gods and objective moral facts, the believer in an independent natural reality which can be and is known in part and to some degree, and which has existed long before, and will exist long after, the existence of life and consciousness. The other Nietzsche also denies gods and objective morality but, as a wild nihilist, further denies the existence of any objective reality at all as well as of facts, of truth, of knowledge, of the objectivity of logic, and so on. This book is primarily about the sober Nietzsche; but part of the reason I see him this way is because I see some other thinkers similarly, especially some of those who think they find in Nietzsche some basis for their own views. I am thinking, for example, of those postmodernists who tell us (as an objective truth?) that science is "just another narrative" with no claim to privilege–that germ theory, for example, is not objectively true, and indeed could not be objectively true because nothing is objectively true. But I would say that in their daily lives, not to mention some of the arguments they make for their views, not only these postmodernists, but also idealists, skeptics, certain kinds of materialists, and all deniers of objective reality and objective truth contradict exactly what they profess to believe. And if, as some such persons do say, they are quite content to allow contradictions as acceptable, then I do not have, and no one else should have, anything more to say to them.

In their *Nietzsche's Perspectivism,* Steven Hales and Rex Welshon express a milder version of my two-Nietzsches suggestion, speaking of "a kind of double movement in Nietzsche" and "both a yes-saying part and a no-saying part" (2000, 8). But they find these somewhat contrary aspects as complementary, in support of which they cite a passage in *Human, All Too Human* in which he says:

> The philosopher believes that the value of his philosophy lies in the whole, in the building: posterity discovers it in the bricks with which he built and which

> are then often used again for better building: in the fact, that is to say, that that building can be destroyed and *nonetheless* possess value as material. (HH "Assorted Opinions and Maxims" 201, Nietzsche's emphasis)

The entry is entitled *Error of Philosophers*, not quoted by Hales and Welshon, and presumably the error is expressed in the first phrase. Granted that, in many ways, there is a constructive Nietzsche and a destructive Nietzsche, and granted that especially the destructive aspect takes a much more extreme form in him than in other philosophers (but in almost all of whom it exists to some degree), I think it is more useful to see Nietzsche as operating on two levels, as it were, rather than on the same level, merely going back and forth in emphasis but with the same basic project. This is all somewhat vague, to be sure; and I am making a stronger point than the fact that Nietzsche, like every philosopher, presupposes an objective world that includes other people as readers, whatever view he is, or could be, expressing. It is that, even acknowledging all of the texts of the destructive sort, Nietzsche in fact puts forth an ontology–an account of how reality is. I think, again despite all of those just-mentioned texts, that Nietzsche really believed the world is the way that his ontology says it is. But attempting to measure a philosopher's (or anyone's) precise degree of belief is generally a futile enterprise, and I am content to say that it is an ontology that is expressed by the texts, whatever else they may express and even granted that some of them may express the impossibility of ontology.

Hales and Welshon are not opposed to ascribing an ontology to Nietzsche, but insist that it must be a "perspectivist ontology" by which they appear to mean that every element as well as every combination of elements of the world is, or maps onto, a perspective. This idea they somehow connect with a bundle theory of objects; confusedly, I think, as I shall try to show in my own discussion of bundle theories in the fourth chapter. But I shall not give much more attention to the perspectivist aspect *of* the ontology (if, indeed, it has one), and I say this even if, in some possibly important sense, it is an ontology *from* a "perspective", and not only in the trivial sense in which everything a person says or does is from a certain location in space and time and society and culture, just because every person has such a location. And I shall have more to say about Nietzsche's perspectivism in general in the next chapter and in the fourth chapter.

That next chapter, the second, has truth and especially objectivity as its main subjects. The third chapter will treat of Nietzsche's theory of constant change, always acknowledged but rarely given significant treatment. Substances and things are the subject of the fourth chapter and minds of the fifth. Although causality is arguably not a fundamental matter of ontology, I shall nonetheless treat Nietzsche's views of it in the sixth chapter. Only in the final, seventh chapter will I discuss the will to power at any length. And with that I will have set out Nietzsche's ontology.

* * *

I am not, by the usual measures, a Nietzsche scholar. I was trained by, and became a colleague of, a member of the Vienna Circle, Gustav Bergmann, who admired Nietzsche in a remote kind of way, especially for his views on religion and morality, but who insisted that he was not worth reading as a serious philosopher. Even so, early in my teaching career, without in the least abandoning my analytic orientation (although not in the sense of so-called conceptual analysis) and mainly because of student interest in Sartre, I began teaching an undergraduate course on existentialist philosophers. It did not take long for me to come to the conclusion that Nietzsche was the most interesting of those who are traditionally put in that category, perhaps just because he fits it so poorly. And toward the end of my teaching years, I decided to do an upperclass/graduate-level course on Nietzsche alone, which I taught four times before my retirement. Furthermore, I wrote but never published a short paper on Nietzsche's ontology, which I have delivered on three occasions. While I have never considered myself, as a philosopher, primarily interested in Nietzsche, I have done what I hope to be sufficient in order to be taken seriously in this essay, not only by anyone with an interest in Nietzsche but also, and especially, by the serious scholars from whom I have learned so much. Reading in the literature, I did become convinced that I had something new and worthwhile to say about Nietzsche; but that will be for others to judge. My contribution, if it be such, is that of using the tools of structural history and analytic ontology in what I believe to be an original way in understanding Nietzsche. And I have rarely hesitated to import my own views, and to argue with Nietzsche, on many important matters. As for the literature, I may say here that the authors I found, overwhelmingly, to be of the most value and interest are Maudemarie Clark, Peter Poellner, John Richardson, Richard Schacht, and Steven Hales and Rex Welshon. Richard Schacht has also been a valuable source of advice and information, for which I express my gratitude.

The final impetus for proceeding on this project came from the Andrew W. Mellon Foundation, which in 2008 named me an Emeritus Faculty Fellow. I am grateful for their confidence in my project as well as their material support.

TRUTH AND OBJECTIVITY

A philosopher's ontology is, or is expressed by, his or her statements of a certain kind; namely, those about certain kinds of fundamental features of reality. To have an ontology, then, would seem to presuppose that the philosopher believes not only that there is a mind-independent reality but that we, or at least he or she, has or can have knowledge or rational belief about that reality. This in turn presupposes that there are truths to be known as well as objective means for discovery of some of those truths. Even the idealist, who holds that in some sense everything is or depends on the mental, agrees that we do not *decide* the nature of reality.

According to a widely-held view, to be found however more among non-philosophers than philosophers, Nietzsche was an ardent opponent of both truth and objectivity. While it is by no means clear what it does or could mean to be an opponent of truth, it could be, and has been, taken to mean or imply that there is no objective reality for there to be truths about; or, more generally, that there are no truthmakers, even given some idea of truth as correspondence. As for objectivity, one can be its opponent both in the sense of denying its possibility and in the sense of denying its desirability; and both senses have been ascribed to Nietzsche.

If this widely-held view is correct, in either or both aspects, then it would seem to be absurd either for Nietzsche to proceed to propose an ontology, or for any commentator to ascribe, on whatever basis, an ontology to him. But this view is not correct–in either aspect. That is my thesis, here to be argued only briefly. More precisely, Nietzsche believed in the correspondence "theory" of truth, and in both the possibility and the desirability of objectivity and the acquisition thereby of knowledge or rational belief. My focus in this brief chapter will be on the somewhat neglected topic of objectivity in Nietzsche, but I shall begin with some discussion of the much more fully treated topic of truth.

What is truth? According to the nearly universal opinion of philosophers, there are various *theories*, each of which attempts to answer that question in a certain way. Traditionally, and systematically according to some, there are three major theories of this sort: the correspondence theory, the coherence theory, and the pragmatic theory. And each of these has been ascribed to Nietzsche. I have a somewhat different initial outlook on this matter of theories of truth, and that is why I put the word 'theory' in double quotes in the preceding paragraph. I would rather say that, as any dictionary will confirm, truth just *is* correspondence, and that the philosophical task is not to uncover its "real" meaning, but to lay bare the ontology of correspondence, which necessarily takes us to a theory of intentionality. Unlike many philosophers, I don't argue about the meanings of words; and the fact of the matter (the anthropological fact, if you like) is that 'true' (to take the adjective) means, according to my office dictionary, "conformable to fact, in accordance with the actual state of things" and "conformable to nature or reality".

Another way to express something like this approach is to distinguish, as Nietzsche himself sometimes but never carefully and consistently did, the *nature* of truth (correspondence) from the *criterion* or *criteria* of truth (coherence, possibly among others), from the *value* of truth (its pragmatic aspects). Nietzsche raised seriously for the first time, and perhaps more deeply than anyone since, the question of the value of truth, often suggesting that the traditional view that humans are always better off, at least in the long run, with truth instead of falsehood is itself an important falsehood.

Everyone believes in the idea of truth as correspondence, insofar as everyone who speaks any natural language means in saying of some belief or sentence that it is true (or whatever the word is in any given language) that that belief or sentence "tells it like it is," that whatever it says or affirms to be the case is the case. Social life would be impossible without some such notion in language, and in English that notion is expressed by the word 'true' although, of course, it can be expressed in other ways. And everyone lives his or her life on the assumption that there is an objective reality of which we have some significant knowledge and of which we can speak by using bits of language that have the property of being true in the sense of correspondence with larger or smaller bits of that reality. Some postmodernists and others may say, and even pretend to believe (because one can only pretend on this matter if that includes pretending to oneself) that "it" is all a matter of "rhetoric" and "narratives" and that, to take an example of their own, the germ theory of disease is "just another narrative," having no more claim to the property of being true than the demon theory or any other. But do these learned academics then not bother having their children vaccinated? Or do they allow their young children to play in the street because, on their view, the scientific account of the effects of fast-moving pieces of metal on the human organism is "just another narrative" alongside the "narrative" that being slammed into by trucks is good for you? These questions answer themselves.

In these respects, Nietzsche is like everyone else. And, in my view, that would be sufficient to proceed. Nietzsche, whatever he and some others have said, believed in a mind-independent reality of which we can have some knowledge. (Even minds themselves, one of my topics, are mind-independent in the crucial sense that their fundamental features do not depend on what anyone believes, desires, values, and so on.) But does that mean that we are simply to dismiss Nietzsche's many criticisms of the notion of truth, at least as he takes it to have been understood traditionally–dismiss them both as being of any inherent sense or value, and also as relevant to the project of ontology? What about all of his talk about "perspectivism" and "interpretation," not to mention his criticisms of scientists in their allegedly naive conception of their work with respect to truth, and his frequent use of double quotes around the word when truth is the topic, and much more? These questions also answer themselves; and we must, therefore, say more. But most of what I want to say will come in my discussion of objectivity.

On the matter of truth in Nietzsche's philosophy, there is little that I or, I daresay, anyone can add to Maudemarie Clark's exhaustive and insightful treatment in her *Nietzsche on Truth and Philosophy,* with her many distinctions and references to texts. But if one does add Richard Schacht's chapter "Truth and Knowledge" in his *Nietzsche* and his essay "Nietzsche-an Cognitivism," one has compelling reasons to say that, at least for the mature Nietzsche, there is no doubt that not only are there truths to be known, but that some of them are known. Both Clark and Schacht trace Nietzsche's thinking on truth and on knowledge from his earliest philosophical publications to his latest, Clark being especially reluctant to rely on the *Nachlass,* and thinking she can make her case with only those works Nietzsche prepared for publication.

(For an important thinker who regards Nietzsche as decisively and correctly (!) rejecting both truth and objectivity in any recognizable sense, see

Gianni Vattimo's *Dialogue With Nietzsche*. His "postmodernist" interpretation and appropriation of what he takes to be Nietzsche's thought about truth and objectivity relies heavily, indeed almost exclusively, on Nietzsche's early writings whereas, it is only fair to add, mine relies with comparable emphasis on his later writings. This difference alludes to my earlier suggestion of a distinction between Nietzsche the wild nihilist and Nietzsche the sober naturalist, but that distinction correlates only loosely with the early Nietzsche and the late Nietzsche.)

Before we turn to the notion of objectivity, there is an aspect of the nature of truth that needs further mention. Without going into technical detail here (see Addis, 1989, 81-86), we may say that truth is fundamentally a property of certain thoughts and derivatively of certain bits of language. But it is not a simple monadic property of those things in that something else must (in the definitional sense) exist in order for any such thing to have that property: in order for the *thought* that light travels at about 300,000 km/sec to be true, there must exist its *truthmaker*, the *fact* that light travels at about 300,000 km/sec, existing independently of the thought. This is, again, the idea of truth as correspondence. But the point to be made here is that any fact or circumstance whatsoever can be a truthmaker, however vague or fleeting, as long as it can be thought of. So the fact, if it is a fact, that there is nothing permanent in reality, the theme of the next chapter, is no barrier to the possibility of truth. One can define, or rather re-define, 'truth' so that it applies only to those thoughts that have unchanging objects as their objects, and then draw the conclusion that because there are no such objects, there is no truth (putting aside that thought itself). But that does not mean that in the ordinary sense of 'truth' there are no truths.

Even given that there are truths to be known and that we know some of them (or at least have true beliefs, perhaps knowing them without knowing that we know them, to allude to some current epistemological discussion), there remains the question of entitlement: whether or not we are ever justified in affirming the truth of some hypothesis and the corresponding falsehood of contrary views. But this question can be taken in importantly different ways, only one of which is the question of objectivity.

One way of answering the question of the possibility of knowledge is that of traditional skepticism, which claims that there is some kind of unconquerable gulf or barrier between the mind and the putative objects of knowledge or that the real world might be radically different from how it seems to be. It might be said, by way of contrast to the other way of approaching the question, that this one, while recognizing that the mind is in any case limited, nevertheless locates the barrier(s) to knowledge in the world itself (never mind how much knowledge must be presupposed in order to make the argument) and not as a defect of the mind. In contrast, the approach that questions the possibility of objectivity in trying to understand the world does precisely that: propose that the human mind is somehow incapable, due to its own nature, of gaining knowledge of the world. This putative defect of the mind is usually assigned to its quality of what we might call being "localized," that is, that every person is necessarily situated in a particular time, place, social class, and culture such that any attempt to understand the world is affected in a deleterious way by the limited perspective that such localization entails. And this idea of localization is, in some form or other, probably the most important sense in which, according to Nietzsche, we always necessarily approach the world from a perspective. Thus, according to this line of thinking, an objective understanding of the world is impossible.

The classical discussion of objectivity concerns the possibility of knowledge of society itself, beginning with the *idéologues* of the post-French Revolution years who were the first to make the important distinction between the *causes* of beliefs and the *reasons* that people give for their beliefs, a distinction that suggests that, in the most important sense, *why* a person believes what he or she does believe is sometimes, often, or even always "outside" the person's consciousness, which in turn suggests that it is difficult or impossible for a person to have beliefs that are rationally grounded. This is the tradition that runs through Hegel, Marx, Dilthey, and, most thoroughly, Karl Mannheim in his classic *Ideology and Utopia.* Mannheim argued, paradoxically invoking vast assumptions of knowledge about social classes and their role in what people believe about society, that knowledge about society was impossible. Indeed, his was a large-scale example of what I regard as the self-refutation of the general thesis of the impossibility of knowledge, whether of society or anything else (see Addis, 1975, 140-142).

The more recent locus of the question of the possibility of objectivity comes from the philosophy of science, especially Thomas Kuhn's *The*

Structure of Scientific Revolutions, in the idea that all cognitive awareness is "theory-laden," thus rendering objective perception or understanding of particular facts impossible. Although Kuhn's thesis is very mild compared to what some of his epigones have claimed to take from it, even in his case one can observe that his argument presupposes the falsity of his conclusion, at least in the general case. By this I mean that while one might argue against objectivity in certain circumstances, perhaps those of theory construction in science, the arguments themselves presuppose that their employer is being objective in the relevant sense. And, in any case, as I shall argue later, the burden of proof is on the one who denies the possibility of objectivity.

But just what *is* this objectivity anyway? Keeping in mind Nietzsche's several references to the importance of method, but independent of that as well, we may say that in the sense here relevant, the property of being objective applies fundamentally, if at all, to method. A *person* is objective if he or she is objective in the *procedure* by which he or she approaches the subject at hand, and the *product* also may be said to be objective under the same condition. Person, procedure, product: the possible objectivity of any of them is best understood if we investigate the idea of objective procedure. To be sure, facts themselves or even the world itself are sometimes said to be objective, meaning most often that they have a nature and an existence that are not dependent on anyone's awareness of them. Objectivity in that sense we are now taking for granted, both in fact and in Nietzsche's opinion, the latter for reasons already given. So the question before us is Nietzsche's view as to the possibility and the desirability of using methods that will give us reasonably grounded beliefs about the world.

But a word about the products, which may be thought of here as bits of knowledge: for an example, the results of the Michelson-Morley experiments (of which Nietzsche could conceivably been aware) that, while formally failed experiments, effectively proved the the constancy of the speed of light and the non-existence of the ether. As Schacht cogently argues, Nietzsche was just not interested in or at least not attracted to the familiar philosophers' idea of knowledge as something of which one has an absolute guarantee of truth (2000, 13-15). If, as I shall argue, Nietzsche believes in the possibility of using methods that qualify as objective, thereby adding to the stock of human knowledge, he most emphatically does not hold that any method gives us unqualified, absolute "certainty" about anything whatsoever. Again, like everyone else, whatever they say, Nietzsche presupposes and agrees that we know many things in the ordinary sense of 'know'; and that is the sense in which the use of certain methods gives us a better chance of being right or more nearly right about how the world is in this or that respect than others, such as revelation or pure reason or magical incantations. In that sense, we may say, at least provisionally, that the Michelson-Morley experiments, because their employers proceeded in an objective manner, gave us some knowledge about light.

In general, Nietzsche's many comments on objectivity, whether or not he uses the word in a particular passage, can be divided into those in which he is critical of what he takes to be a naive conception of objectivity, especially among scientists, on the one hand and, on the other hand, those in which he endorses the possibility and value of objective methods against most philosophers, especially idealists, as well as, and most of all, against religionists and moralists. There are many passages with which I could begin my argument, but I shall start with one of my favorite passages in Nietzsche, which is from one of his last works. In *Twilight of the Idols*, Nietzsche writes:

> My recreation, my preference, my *cure* from all Platonism has always been *Thucydides.* Thucydides and, perhaps, Machiavelli's *Principe* are most closely related to myself by the unconditional will not to gull oneself and to see reason in *reality*–not in "reason," still less in "morality." For the wretched embellishment of the Greeks into an ideal, which the "classically educated" youth carries into life as a prize for his classroom drill, there is no more complete cure than Thucydides. One must follow him line by line and read no less clearly between the lines: there are few thinkers who say so much between the lines. With him the culture of the Sophists, by which I mean the culture of the realists, reaches its perfect expression–this inestimable movement amid the moralistic and idealistic swindle set loose on all sides by the Socratic schools. Greek philosophy: the decadence of the Greek instinct. Thucydides: the great sum, the last revelation of that strong, severe, hard factuality which was instinctive with the older Hellenes. In the end, it is *courage* in the face of reality that distinguishes a man like Thucydides from Plato: Plato is a coward before reality, consequently he flees into the ideal; Thucydides has control of *himself*, consequently he also maintains control of things. (TI "What I Owe to the Ancients" 2, Nietzsche's emphases)

"[T]hat strong, severe, hard factuality" (*jener starken, strengen, harten Tatsächlichkeit*)–this beautiful expression captures perfectly what I take Nietzsche to be talking about while expressing one of his highest values. Furthermore, the passage makes abundantly clear (1) that this way of approaching reality is possible, (2) that this way of approaching reality is highly desirable, but (3) that this way of approaching reality is difficult. And yet Thucydides succeeded; his objectivity is most strongly evidenced by the facts (as every reader of *History of the Peloponnesian War* can tell for him- or herself), first, that he was highly conscious of the nature of his approach in that he *chose* and *strove* to be objective and, second, that (keeping in mind that he was Athenian and had even been a general, though exiled for an important loss on the battlefield), the reader cannot tell from his *History* which side, if either, he wanted to win.

This passage also makes clear that, while Nietzsche sometimes lapses into the cosmic mode, especially in his criticisms of the ideal of objectivity, he (rightly) thinks of it as something that people possess in degrees and more in some circumstances than others, that it is something, at least in formal contexts like writing history, that must be intended, but that some cultures make its expression more likely than others, some so much perhaps that it is a matter of "instinct," as the passage almost says. (Perhaps it would be better to say, following Aristotle, in whom there is some recovery of that naturalistic approach that Plato had opposed, that, for some people, proceeding objectively is "second nature.") But we may assume that, for Nietzsche, even in the best of circumstances only a few people are objective and only some of the time. It may be agreed that no one is, or can be, wholly objective, whatever exactly that would mean, but that tells against neither the possibility nor the desirability of being as objective as possible when the cause of knowledge is before us.

For the philosopher, it is especially important to try to understand and to perceive the world objectively, even if the overwhelming majority of philosophers not only fail to do so but, according to Nietzsche, oppose those who try. For example, in *Beyond Good and Evil,* he writes of what is necessary for the discovery of truth by the philosopher:

> But there is no doubt at all that the evil and unhappy are more favored when it comes to the discovery of certain *parts* of truth, and that the probability of their success here is greater–not to speak of the evil who are happy, a species the moralists bury in silence. Perhaps hardness and cunning furnish more favorable

conditions for the origin of the strong, independent spirit and philosopher than that gentle, fine, conciliatory good-naturedness and art of taking things lightly which people prize, and prize rightly, in a scholar. Assuming first of all that the concept "philosopher" is not restricted to the philosopher who writes books–or makes books of *his* philosophy.

A final trait for the image of the free-spirited philosopher is contributed by Stendahl whom, considering German taste, I do not want to fail to stress–for he goes against the German taste. *"Pour être bon philosophe,"* says this last great psychologist, *"il faut être sec, clair, sans illusion. Un banquier, qui a fait fortune, a une partie du caractère requis pour faire des découvertes en philosophie, c'est-à-dire pour voir clair dans ce qui est."* [In order to be a good philosopher, it is necessary to be dry, clear, without illusion. A banker, who has made a fortune, has a characteristic required for making philosophical discoveries; namely, to see clearly into that which is]. (BGE 39, Nietzshche's emphases, my translation from the French)

But how does a philosopher acquire this trait? In a late note (WP 425), Nietzsche summarizes some attitudes one must adopt, ones that have often been mentioned and alluded to in his published writings:

"Objectivity" in the philosopher: moral indifference toward oneself, blindness toward good or ill consequences: lack of scruples about using dangerous means; perversity and multiplicity of character considered and exploited as an advantage.
My profound indifference toward myself: I desire no advantage from my insights and do not avoid the disadvantages that accompany them.—Here I include what might be called *corruption* of the character; this perspective is beside the point: I use my character, but try neither to understand nor to change it—the personal calculus of virtue has not entered my head for a moment. It seems to me that one shuts the door on knowledge as soon as one becomes interested in one's own case–or, worse, the "salvation of one's soul"!— One must not take one's morality too seriously and not let oneself be deprived of a modest right to its opposite— (KGW VIII 11 [300], Nietzsche's emphasis)

Morality is indeed to be overcome if one is to be objective. As Nietzsche says in a nice phrase in *Beyond Good and Evil* of the psychologist (such as himself) who would see the world without illusion: "We sail right *over* morality" (BGE 23, Nietsche's emphasis). But it is time to say more clearly, though succinctly, just what it is to adopt objective methods in the pursuit of truth before we see further what Nietzsche had to say about methods.

If a person wants to investigate some matter objectively, he or she must be prepared, as we say, to pursue the truth whatever it may be and wherever it may lead. This means, as we just saw, putting aside one's values (except, of course, for the value of objectivity itself and whatever it implies), one's hopes, one's desires, and in general anything about oneself that might incline one to finding, or imagining oneself to have found, a certain outcome. It may also involve taking various "perspectives" (about which more later, in Nietzsche's somewhat special senses) on the subject of investigation, in order to obtain a fuller grasp of the subject; the use of instruments and other tools that diminish the direct role of the investigator in observation or that enhance the probability of accurate perception; and, perhaps most of all, the conscious intention to try to get at things as they are, whatever one may wish them to be. But, I would say, somewhat differently from Nietzsche, that a person *may* well proceed objectively–from either "second nature" or even original disposition--without thinking of oneself as doing so.

I now want to make a crucial logical point against those, from whatever quarter, say that it is not possible for a person to be objective, and that all theories are biased or distortions of reality or the like. Consider again Thucydides as well as Michelson and Morley, the first mainly, but not exclusively, concerned with description, that latter mainly, but not exclusively, with explanation. If someone now says that these investigators were not objective in their projects, let us inquire for that person's reasons. If the reply is that no one can be objective, I ask what the evidence is for that, given these, and numerous other, apparent examples to the contrary. Just exactly where is the bias and the resulting distortion in the results? I submit that the only way that the general thesis of the impossibility of objectivity can be established, or, rather, *seem* to be established, is by induction. And that involves taking every theory or history or whatever, *one by one*, and displaying the distortion. Not only will such an undertaking fail miserably but–and here is the crucial point, already alluded to–such an undertaking presupposes that this meta-investigator is himself or herself proceeding objectively, that in locating bias and distortion he or she is proceeding in a way that eliminates or at least minimizes bias and distortion. I made this point against Mannheim earlier on, who uses his vast knowledge of social classes and social reality in order to argue that knowledge of society is impossible (even if, on his view, the "free intelligentsia," with their only loose attachment to the traditional classes, may obtain somewhat clearer views—an attempt by Mannheim to diminish the tensions of his theory).

Needless to say, it is not difficult to find examples of theories and histories in which bias is all too evident. But any argument that because some theorists are not objective, no theorists are objective is as bad an argument as that because some theorists are not women, no theorists are women, especially given that there very much seem to be clear examples of theorists who are objective and of theorists who are women. And if, independent of, and even contrary to the empirical evidence, someone thinks he or she can establish the generalization that no one is objective, let us hear the argument–although I can't imagine what it could possibly be. The fact is that much of the contemporary railing against objectivity by postmodernists, certain kinds of feminists, and others is itself ideological thinking–that is, thinking in which their values distort their ability to grasp and to accept the reality.

But with that, let us look further at what Nietzsche says about method–the heart of the matter. Turning first to a passage in *The Antichrist*, we read:

> The most valuable insights are discovered last; but the most valuable insights are the *methods*. *All* the methods, *all* the presuppositions of our current scientific outlook, were opposed for thousands of years with the most profound contempt. For their sake, men were excluded from the company of "decent" people and considered "enemies of God," despisers of the truth, and "possessed." Anyone with a scientific bent was a Chandala.
> We have had the whole pathos of mankind against us–their conception of what truth *ought* to be: every "thou shalt" has hitherto been aimed against us. Our objectives, our practice, our quiet, cautious, mistrustful manner—all these were considered utterly unworthy and contemptible. (A 13, Nietzsche's emphases)

(In a closely similar passage in the notebooks—(KGW VI/5)—Nietzsche writes not of "our objectives" (*Unsre Objekte*) as above, but instead of "our objectivity" (*unsre Objectivität*) and translated as such by Kaufmann in WP 469.)

Here as elsewhere Nietzsche sees objectivity, first, as a matter of method, but also as something to be *achieved*, something to be pursued against religion and morality. For then as now, many will accept, or ignore, science as long as its results do not contradict their values and beliefs and hopes. But when they do, then the method of science, broadly conceived, itself comes under attack.

Although he doesn't use the word in the part I shall quote, a passage in *Twilight of the Idols* speaks, in the context of education, of training to be objective (although, ironically, at the end of the entry Nietzsche contrasts what he approves of to 'the famous modern "objectivity"'):

> I put forward at once–lest I break with my style, which is *affirmative* and deals with contradiction and criticism only as a means, only involuntarily–the three tasks for which educators are required. One must learn to *see*, one must learn to *think*, one must learn to *speak* and *write*: the goal in all three is a noble culture. Learning to *see*–accustoming the eye to calmness, to patience, to letting things come up to it; postponing judgment, learning to go around and grasp each individual case from all sides. That is the *first* preliminary schooling for spirituality: not to react at once to a stimulus, but to gain control of all the inhibiting, excluding instincts. Learning to *see*, as I understand it, is almost what, unphilosophically speaking, is called a strong will: the essential feature is precisely *not* to "will"–to *be able* to suspend decision. (TI "What the Germans Lack" 6, Nietzsche's emphases)

Again we understand that objectivity (whether or not Nietzsche would call it that in this context) is something to be achieved, something for which one can be trained, something that educators can (as many do, so I say) impart to their students. Being objective, at least by intention, may require a "strong will" in the sense of preventing oneself from jumping to unwarranted conclusions, especially–in the case of judgments about individual things–those based on questionable generalizations or initial impressions or limited perspectives.

Every likely reader of this essay will know that there is much discussion in Nietzsche's writings (though more in his unpublished than published) about perspectivism and interpretation, and, further, that these discussions have often been used to support the thesis that Nietzsche was an opponent of the possibility and probably also the desirability of objectivity in the pursuit of knowledge (although these same people would probably also say that Nietzsche denies the possibility of knowledge). And it would be foolish to deny that there are many passages in Nietzsche's writings that can reasonably be used to support the thesis. At the least, it might be said that, however one ultimately regards Nietzsche on these matters, he gives some reasons and arguments that could be used to deny the possibility of objectivity. I cannot undertake, and need not undertake, a substantive discussion of this matter beyond what I have already said, except to take note of one of the most important passages in Nietzsche where he directly examines the topic of perspectives and objectivity. It occurs in *On the Genealogy of Morals* in which the context is his discussion of ascetic self-contempt as applied to the realms of truth and reason, particularly in the idea of using reason to oppose reason, this passage being, I submit, the single most important one in Nietzsche's published writings, and perhaps all of his writings, on objectivity, perspectives, interpretations, and knowledge:

> But precisely because we seek knowledge, let us not be ungrateful to such resolute reversals of accustomed perspectives and valuations with which the spirit has, with apparent mischievousness and futility, raged against itself for so long: to see differently in this way for once, to *want* to see differently, is no small discipline and preparation of the intellect for its future "objectivity"—the latter understood not as "contemplation without interest" (which is a nonsensical absurdity), but as the ability *to control* one's Pro and Con and to dispose of them, so that one knows how to employ a *variety* of perspectives and affective interpretations in the service of knowledge.
>
> . . .
>
> There is *only* a perspective seeing, *only* a perspective "knowing"; and the *more* eyes, different eyes, we can use to observe one thing, the more complete will our "concept" of this thing, our "objectivity," be. But to eliminate the will altogether, to suspend each and every affect, supposing we were capable of this–what would that mean but to *castrate* the intellect?-- (GM II 12, Nietzsche's emphases)

Here Nietzsche affirms some version of perspectivism and the necessity of interpretations; but far from giving these as reasons for denying objectivity and resulting knowledge, he sees them as partly constitutive of objective method and "in the service of knowledge." Furthermore, being objective is a matter of *self-discipline*–controlling one's "Pro and Con"–one of Nietzsche's highest values, especially as expressed in his ideal of the *Übermensch*. I have suggested, as Nietzsche has also at least hinted, that such self-discipline can become a matter of second nature, and that, as applied to the idea of "higher types," some cultures more than others encourage such types.

To be sure, some of the quoted passage takes things farther than I would like, and I have included the second part to make clear that, in this same context, Nietzsche seems to have done so. Perspective "seeing" (even understood broadly), yes; perspective "knowing", perhaps, but only in the sense that what we in fact know depends on our location in time and society and much more that is not universal to the species. How I came to know that light travels at almost exactly 300,000 km/sec depends on much about me (my "perspective" if you like), but the *truth* of that piece of knowledge in wholly independent of me. I am not entirely certain that Nietzsche clearly made that distinction or even that, if it were made to him, he would agree with it as made. But I am certain that Nietzsche was not a relativist of facts as he was of values. (Some have denied that he was a relativist of values too; for example, Richard Schacht. But when that is exactly the issue, as in *The Twilight of the Idols* "The Improvers of Mankind 1, Nietzsche contrasts the absence of "realities" in the case of values with that of factual matters. Schacht's discussion of objectivity in his *Making Sense of Nietzsche* is almost wholly concerned with the matter of values, but his understanding of the passage quoted above, as expressed in his *Nietzsche* (1983, 9-10) is similar to mine.)

But before I conclude this chapter, it would be well to say something more about Nietzsche's perspectivism or, rather, his various meanings or versions of it. Perhaps others have cut things even finer, but I identify five different ideas or themes in Nietzsche that he sometimes describes as involving (only) a perspective that we humans have on the world, and usually in a way that implies a limitation, but not necessarily one that cannot be, at least in some measure, overcome. Very broadly speaking, we can distinguish those aspects or themes that distinguish humans from each other from those that do not, the former being generally more interesting and more important. Far and away the most important of either sort is what I above called the theme of localization, a theme to be found in many important nineteenth-century thinkers but, at least in one form, most fully sounded in the work of the twentieth-century thinker, Karl Mannheim. This theme I discussed briefly above, and here I will add only that, while the argument against objectivity for most of these other thinkers rested on the alleged necessary limitations on us due to being members of certain traditional social classes, this kind of localization as such plays little or no role in Nietzsche's thought. I say 'as such' because the forms of localization that do matter to Nietzsche are not unrelated to social class, but have to do directly more with religious and philosophical beliefs, values, and temporal and spatial location (that is, the time and place at which one lives), none of which is wholly independent of social class. I have already argued that any *argument* to the conclusion that localization, of whatever form, necessarily prevents objective understanding and knowledge presupposes the falsehood of that conclusion, and so is to be rejected.

A somewhat distinct theme concerns the different "approaches" people take in trying to understand things. I am thinking in particular of Nietzsche's distinction between those who would "approach" their subjects by way of generalizations as contrasted with those who "approach" each subject as individual and possibly unique. Nietzsche, as we know, endorses the latter, and considers it to be a component of objectivity, even if, in some sense, it is a certain "perspective".

A third conception that does or may distinguish among humans with respect to their perspectives relates to the different ways to categorize the phenomena. This is a more technical matter than that of localization, and underlies some of the contemporary discussion of realism and anti-realism. It is also a theme that appears in some anthropological literature, often being used to cast doubt on the possibility of objectivity (which, in any case, is a common theme in that field, usually in the cause of not being offensive to other cultures but almost entirely lacking in intellectual sophistication).

Of the notions of perspective that have more to do with humans in general, as contrasted with other kinds of beings (actual or possible), Nietzsche mentions, first, the fact that we have senses of a certain kind that allow us only a partial grasp, by that means, of the world, knowing that other animals have somewhat different perceptions of it. Here we may note once more that the idea of this kind of perspective rests on knowledge of a certain kind, knowledge that, at least in this context, itself appears to be objectively obtained. And that very knowledge makes it possible for us to know how to treat the fact that, in this sense, we have only one of many possible perspectives on reality and also how to "overcome" that circumstance.

Finally, there are human needs of a certain kind, which collectively distinguish us from other beings, actual and possible. Above all, as far as Nietzsche is concerned, we need to have certain crucial *beliefs* in order to get about in the world, beliefs that are almost certainly false to the extent that they presuppose a reality of a certain structure. In this sense, our "perspective" on the world is false, according to Nietzsche, but so, we may assume, is any alternative to it. And while it is this notion of perspective that might seem especially to contradict any possibility of objectively obtained knowledge of an objective reality, we may notice once more that it rests on presumed knowledge of us and that reality.

And now I am ready to generalize that point. Just as Mannheim's arguments against the possibility of objective knowledge of society presuppose a huge body of objective knowledge of society, Nietzsche's various conceptions of perspective and other actual and apparent objections he sometimes makes against the possibility of knowledge of the world presuppose a huge body of presumed knowledge of that world and our place in it. More generally, but also more precisely, they presuppose a certain ontology, a certain more or less consistent view about the nature of reality and about human beings, the former especially with respect to change, substances and things, causation, and the will to power, the latter especially with respect to the nature and efficacy of the mind. So even for those who insist that for Nietzsche there is no truth, no knowledge, no objective procedures, and possibly no objective reality to begin with, I say that what may seem to be arguments in Nietzsche for those views rest on a certain ontology. Regard this as paradoxical or even contradictory, if you like; but it invites us in any case to examine the ontology, whatever its epistemological status.

With this admittedly somewhat brief discussion of truth, knowledge, and especially objectivity in Nietzsche, I am nevertheless prepared to conclude that his views of these matters are no obstacle to his having an ontology, that is, some general views about the nature of reality, which he could consistently, if not always plausibly, claim to know. Of course, being objective is neither a necessary nor a sufficient condition for getting to, or close to, the truth. It is not sufficient because there is no method that, no matter how carefully followed, guarantees that one will get it right; and not necessary because of the fact that unreliable methods, such as prophecy, may occasionally by chance get something right. So Nietzsche, like all rational people, proceeds on the assumption that some ways of trying to get at how things are have a better chance of succeeding than others, always recognizing the limitations of the human mind but without despairing at the fact that we shall never know everything nor, perhaps, anything in its totality, whatever the "it" is. On the contrary, far from being a cause for despair, the search for knowledge, for Nietzsche, is quite the opposite, as he expresses it in this exuberant passage from *The Gay Science:*

> *In media vita* [In mid-life].—No, life has not disappointed me. On the contrary, I find it truer, more desirable and mysterious every year—ever since the day when the great liberator came to me: the idea that life could be an experiment of the seeker for knowledge—and not a duty, not a calamity, not trickery. —And knowledge itself: let it be something else for others; for example, a bed to rest on, or the way to such a bed, or a diversion, or a form of leisure—for me it is a world of dangers and victories in which heroic feelings, too, find places to dance and play. *"Life as a means to knowledge"*—with this principle in one's heart one can live not only boldly but even gaily, and laugh gaily, too. And who knows how to laugh anyway and live well if he does not first know a good deal about war and victory? (GS 324, Nietzsche's emphases)

Let us investigate Nietzsche's ontology.

CONSTANT CHANGE

We begin the ideas of *being* and *becoming*, for these underlie Nietzsche's theory of constant change. And it is natural, given the history of Western philosophy, to speak, following Plato, of the *worlds* of being and becoming although, as we shall see, Nietzsche draws the distinction in a somewhat more radical way. In general, as in Plato, the world of being is one of eternal objects–eternal in the sense of being altogether "outside" space and time. Those eternal objects for Plato are what are called the *forms* and sometimes, misleadingly, the *ideas*–misleading because they are in no sense whatsoever mental things. Be that as it may, there are, in the history of philosophy and religion, many versions of a world of eternal objects, the other most important being that of gods, angels, and souls. (We know that such things are in fact often described, in this or that myth, as changing; but officially, as it were, at least the god of the monotheists is an eternal object in the sense indicated.) And of course there are other versions of a *two-worlds* view of reality–one that is eternal and unchanging, another that involves change.

That other world is, needless to say, our world of everyday experience. It is a world of becoming, as many philosophers use the word, because in it, unlike the world of being, things come into existence. They become. And of course, they also change and pass out of existence. This world is, of necessity, one of *time*, for there can be no coming into, and passing out of, existence without the passage of time. It is, perhaps, possible that the world of time (and space) is eternal as a whole, so to speak; that is, that it has always existed and always will exist, even though each of the particular things in it, from stars to organisms, comes into existence at a particular time and ceases to exist at a particular time. But that is a somewhat different sense of 'eternal' from that in which the world of being is said to be eternal. That sense is that of existing "outside" space and time, and so admitting no possibility of change, or coming into and passing out of existence in any of its "parts". The other is that of, while being a world of space and time and of change and becoming, has no beginning and no end as a whole. In any case, what fundamentally distinguishes a world of being from a world of becoming is that in the latter, but not in the former, there is *time* and *change*.

But do the things and events in the world of becoming not also have being? Do they not exist just as much as the putative entities of the world of being? The short answer is, in my opinion, yes. But the full answer is much more complicated, and depends, among other things, on the answers one gives to two fundamental questions: (1) Is there in fact a world of eternal objects, a world of being, as we have been speaking so far? (2) If there is such a world, does it have, in some important ontological sense, a greater status than the world of becoming? Of course, if one answers the first question in the negative, then the answer to the second is moot. But almost all philosophers who have answered the first question in the affirmative have also answered the second question in the affirmative: there is, according to these philosophers, in addition to the everyday world of time and change, another world of eternal objects–whether forms or gods or something else–and that other world is not only a "better" world than the world of time and change, but also has *more reality* than the world of time and change. Indeed, according to these same philosophers, its greater reality is such that only that world of eternal objects deserves to be called a world of *being*. And according to some (but not all) of these same philosophers, the world of time and change not only lacks being in the sense in which the eternal world has being, but is only an imperfect "shadow" of the eternal world or, for the most extreme of these philosophers, some kind of illusion in which time and change do not really exist even in a weak sense.

But some philosophers, myself included, maintain that the idea that some things have a "higher reality" than others in the sense of a greater degree of being or existence makes no sense, and this whether the things be eternal or temporal. To be sure, some things have a more fleeting existence than others and, possibly, some things may have a permanent existence, in some sense or other. But a thing either exists or it doesn't exist, whether at a time or eternally. Being in the sense of existence does not admit of degrees in the ontological sense. If that is so, then labeling the putative world of eternal things the world of being while denying being to the world of time and change is, at the least, misleading or, more likely, false or meaningless. And some philosophers who hold the two-worlds view of reality are quite content to allow that the inhabitants of those two worlds do have existence to the same degree and in the same sense, even if in the one case it is eternal and in the other temporary.

But, as one might say, the damage was done–by Plato, above all. And Western philosophy has had to live ever since with the notion that, if there is a world of eternal objects at all, it has being while the everyday world of time and change has "only" becoming. And this has fed the further idea, as we saw briefly in the last chapter, that truth, the "real" truth, as some would say, is about only the world of being; that truth being eternal, it can be about only eternal objects. And this, we also saw there, is a mistake. For the sense in which truth *might* be said to be eternal (see Addis 1989, 82) does not require that what truths are *about*–that is, what makes them truths–also be eternal. The *truth* that Charles Lindberg crossed the Atlantic Ocean by plane in 1932, whether itself said to be eternal or not, is about, and made a truth by, the *fact* of Lindberg's crossing the Atlantic Ocean by plane in 1932; and that event, by involving motion also obviously involves time and change as well as having a distinct beginning and end. Unfortunately, on this point it is not only the tradition he was attacking that was confused, but Nietzsche himself never was or became unequivocally clear. But he is quite clear in his contempt for the belief in, and love for, the world of being and its corresponding disparaging of the world of becoming as most philosophers, since Plato, have held, as this lengthy passage in *Twilight of the Idols* make very clear:

> You ask me which of the philosophers' traits are really idiosyncracies? For example, their lack of historical sense, their hatred of the very idea of becoming, their Egypticism. They think that they show their *respect* for a subject when they de-historicize it, *sub specie aeterni*–when they turn it into a mummy. . . . Death, change, old age, as well as procreation and growth, are to their minds objections--even refutations. Whatever has being does not become; whatever becomes does not have being. Now they all believe, desperately even, in what has being. But since they never grasp it, they seek for reasons why it is kept from them. "There must be mere appearance, there must be some deception which prevents us from perceiving that which has being: where is the deceiver?"
> "We have found him," they cry ecstatically; "it is the senses! These senses, which are so immoral in other ways too, deceive us concerning the *true* world. Moral: let us free ourselves from the deception of the senses, from becoming, from history, from lies; history is nothing but faith in the senses, faith in lies. Moral: let us say No to all who have faith in the senses, to all the rest of mankind; they are all 'mob.' Let us be philosophers! Let us be mummies! Let us represent monotono-theism by adopting the expression of a gravedigger! And above all, away with the body, this wretched *idée fixe* of the senses, disfigured by all the fallacies of logic, refuted, even impossible, although it is impudent

enough to behave as if it were real!" (TI "'Reason' in Philosophy" 1, Nietzsche's emphases).

While in his early philosophical writings Nietzsche might be said still to be somewhat attracted to the idea of another world than the everyday one–a world, that is, of eternal objects–he eventually, in any case, becomes vehement in his rejection of such a world. For him, there is only the everyday world of time and change, indeed of *constant change*, as we shall eventually see. In the many passages in which this view is expressed, this one from *Twilight of the Idols* shows not only his intellectual rejection of, but also his moral disdain for, the idea of a world in addition to the everyday world of time and change. In this passage, Nietzsche appropriately uses, with irony, the language that so many philosophers of the two-worlds persuasion have used of 'appearance' and 'reality', encompassing the idea once again that the world of time and change is, at best, a "mere" appearance (and a faulty one at that) of the world of genuine reality, that of eternal objects. And he closes the passage with reference to a theme of some of his earliest philosophical writing, especially *The Birth of Tragedy*; namely, that of the tragic artist:

> *First proposition.* The reasons for which "this" world has been characterized as "apparent" are the very reasons which indicate its reality; any other kind of reality is absolutely indemonstrable.
> *Second proposition.* The criteria which have bestowed on the "true being" of things are the criteria of not-being, of *naught*; the "true world" has been constructed out of contradiction to the actual world: indeed an apparent world, insofar as it is merely a moral-optical illusion.
> *Third proposition.* To invent fables about a world "other" than this one has no meaning at all, unless an instinct of slander, detraction, and suspicion against life has gained the upper hand in us: in that case, we avenge ourselves against life with a phantasmagoria of "another," a "better" life.
> *Fourth proposition.* Any distinction between a "true" and an "apparent" world–whether in the Christian manner or in the manner of Kant (in the end, an underhanded Christian)–is only a suggestion of decadence, a symptom of the *decline of life*. That the artist esteems appearance higher than reality is no objection to this proposition. For "appearance" in this case means reality *once more*, only by way of selection, reinforcement, and correction. The tragic artist is no pessimist: he is precisely the one who says Yes to everything questionable, even to the terrible–he is *Dionysian*. (TI "'Reason' in Philosophy" 6, Nietzsche's emphases)

Nietzsche might, therefore, be said to be, in one good sense, a *naturalist* insofar as he believes that the natural world is the only world there is. And this is as good a place as any to say something about Nietzsche's naturalism in other senses as well. I want to discuss this matter in connection with Richard Schacht's ideas about it, and especially with respect to his recently-published essay called "Nietzsche's Anti-Scientistic Naturalism" in which he formulates a detailed and subtle account of what he takes to be the nature of that naturalism, mainly against the views of Brian Leiter as they appear in his *Nietzsche on Morality*. In brief, while Leiter regards Nietzsche's naturalism as consisting primarily in the idea that all legitimate explanations of the phenomena are scientific, causal ones, Schacht insists that, while Nietzsche certainly has respect for such explanations, he also holds that there are other kinds of legitimate explanations or accounts, in particular of human cultural phenomena.

Schacht puts the label of "scientistic" to views of the sort that Leiter ascribes to Nietzsche while calling the view he himself finds in Nietzsche "scientian". This latter adjective is supposed to capture the idea that, while Nietzsche is favorably disposed to science, he does not regard it as the sole source or kind of our understanding of human affairs. Both agree, of course, that Nietzsche wholly, not to say passionately, rejects putative supernatural or other-world explanations of anything whatsoever, for there is no world but our everyday, temporal one for Nietzsche, as we have just been emphasizing.

They are also in agreement on the more specific thesis that, for Nietzsche, humans are part of nature, indeed of the animal realm, in their origin and essential characteristics. But humans have come a long way from their origins; and the richness and varieties of their cultures present us with phenomena that, according to Schacht's reading of Nietzsche, do not yield easily or perhaps at all to scientific, causal explanations; instead they call for, what are here and there given by Nietzsche, accounts of a different character. Of these accounts that Schacht discusses, there are two kinds, which I shall call *developmental* and *interpretive*. (Schacht also calls the one kind developmental.) Developmental accounts are particularly relevant to the facts of emergence and increasing complexity in human affairs, while interpretive accounts go to the phenomenon of meaning.

Schacht presents his arguments and textual evidence in the context of "rescuing" Nietzsche from scientism, just as he has, so Schacht says, earlier had to have been rescued from the "charges" of proto-Nazism, of existentialism, and of post-structuralism. I am happy to join Schacht in this rescue effort, agreeing with him that Nietzsche is not a naturalist in Leiter's sense of allowing only scientific, causal explanations as legitimate ones, but is a naturalist in holding that, while not all legitimate accounts are scientific, causal ones, all legitimate accounts of anything whatsoever must be this-worldly, relying only on facts and events of the only world there is, our everyday, commonsense world, as elaborated by science. But I do not wholly agree with Schacht as to the nature of developmental and interpretive accounts and their relation to scientific, causal ones. And I further hold that there are yet other kinds of legitimate explanations that are not scientific, causal ones than the ones Schacht discusses.

This is not the place for detail, but it can be argued (as I have, 1975, 97-103) that developmental accounts, if they are not lawful (and therefore causal) ones, are simply historical narratives—valuable as such, to be sure, but not explanations. If, on the other hand, they are explanations by way of invoking, explicitly or implicitly, putative developmental laws, there arises the question of whether or not there really are any such laws and, if so, whether or not they are, in a strong sense, reducible to ordinary causal laws. But in either case, developmental accounts may well at least allude to, or presuppose, ordinary causal laws, especially those that have to do with the lawful relations of mind, brain, and behavior.

As for interpretive accounts, I again doubt not their value but their explanatory nature. Following Nietzsche's claim of the impotence of science in understanding a piece of music (GS 373), we can talk, as we well might, of "explaining" the meaning of Richard Wagner's *Der Ring des Niebelungen*, for example; but I would, when I have my philosophical druthers, say instead that we are *describing*, not explaining, the meaning. (I chose this example in mind of Schacht's and Philip Kitcher's interpretation in their *Finding an Ending: Reflections on Wagner's Ring*, easily the best study of Wagner's great work.) Interpretations may well play a role in explanations, but they are not themselves explanations.

Finally, I would maintain that there are, even within science proper, explanations that are not causal ones; namely, *dispositional* explanations (although, or so I have argued, such explanations rest on the possibility of causal explanations—see Addis, 1981). But this is a technical matter of later philosophy of science and not to be found at all in Nietzsche. Be all of this as it may, I express my emphatic agreement with Schacht against Leiter that for Nietzsche (and in fact), there are modes of understanding (whether or not, very strictly speaking, all are modes of explanation) that are not scientific, causal ones and that, therefore, we should adopt Schacht's view of him as scientian, not scientistic.

To summarize my view, but going somewhat beyond the discussion above: Nietzsche *is* a naturalist in holding that (1) there is no supernatural reality, (2) empirical science is a valuable and perhaps the pre-eminent source of knowledge of reality, and (3) human beings are part of nature in their origin and essential characteristics. Nietzsche is *not* a naturalist in holding that (1) natural reality is not wholly material (as I shall argue later); there is a dualism of mind and matter, (2) human reality involves emergent properties that are not ontologically reducible to those that physical science studies, and (3) there are modes of explanation and understanding reality that are not scientific, causal ones.

Finally, with Schacht perhaps in disagreement but with my making no argument here, I would say that Nietzsche's naturalism as just characterized is fully consistent with causal determinism and, as I shall argue later, that Nietzsche in fact is a determinist. But with that, let us return to the topic of constant change.

The theory of constant change–that in the everyday world everything is always changing–does not originate with Nietzsche. Nor, of course, does he claim that it does. In particular, he cites, many times, Heraclitus as his most important progenitor, even if Heraclitus's follower, Cratylus of Athens, is a clearer example among the ancients of a philosopher who advocated the theory and, furthermore, Heraclitus himself gave at least equal importance to the unity of all things amid the constant change, something that Nietzsche held, if at all, only in a quite different sense. Nietzsche does not anywhere develop the theory of constant change, but alludes to it now and again. For example, in *Twilight of the Idols*, where the context is mostly that of the reliability of the senses, and the question of whether or not the everyday world is all there is and the tendency of philosophers to denigrate the world of becoming, Nietzsche writes:

> With the highest respect, I except the name of *Heraclitus.* When the rest of the philosophic folk rejected the testimony of the senses because they showed multiplicity and change, he rejected their testimony because they showed things as if they had permanence and unity. Heraclitus too did the senses an injustice. They lie neither in the way the Eleatics believed, nor as he believed–they do not lie at all. What we *make* of their testimony, that alone introduces lies; for example, the lie of unity, the lie of thinghood, of substance, of permanence. "Reason" is the cause of our falsification of their testimony of the senses. Insofar as the senses show becoming, passing away, and change, they do not lie. But Heraclitus will remain eternally right with his assertion that being is an empty fiction. The "apparent" world is the only one: the "true" world is merely added by a lie. (TI "'Reason' in Philosophy" 2, Nietzsche's emphases)

The primary, direct, ontological reason that Nietzsche has for holding the theory of constant change comes from his radical rejection of anything that implies, or seems to imply, any degree of permanence. This, of course, is very much connected with his rejection of *substance,* which I will treat separately in the next chapter. For, in addition to his contempt for any idea of a *world* of being, of eternal objects, he has a similar distaste for the idea of a *thing* with being *within* the world of becoming, that is, something that remains unchanged through any duration of time; indeed, so much so that he does not really want to speak of *things* at all, with what he takes to be the implication of some degree of permanence in that word. Any commitment to such an entity likewise betrays some kind of disrespect for becoming itself, an unwillingness to let go of the idea of permanence, and even a hatred of change and life itself.

But I want to discuss Nietzsche's views, as far as possible, independent of his moral objections, an approach that he would, at least in some contexts, heartily approve. And while, surely, Nietzsche's first factual (as opposed to normative) suggestion as to why we should not believe in entities with at least some degree of permanence would be that there is no good reason to suppose their existence (the onus of proof always being on the one who affirms, not the one who doubts, the existence of something or other), there is something of an argument in one of his notes of summer 1885 (WP 1062) to the effect that the world of becoming itself, in any case, could not have even momentary lack of change. The context is that of denying any telelogical features of the world:

> If the world had a goal, it must have been reached. If there were for it some unintended final state, this also must have been reached. If it were in any way capable of a pausing and becoming fixed, of "being," if in the whole course of its becoming it possessed even for a moment this capability of "being," then all becoming would long since have come to an end, along with all thinking, all "spirit." The fact of "spirit" as a form of becoming proves that the world has no goal, no final state, and is incapable of being. (KGW VII 35 [15]).

But that, clearly, is not the same as saying that there could not be entities within the world of becoming, whose overall state was always qualitatively different from instant to instant, that remain unchanged for some period of time. Yet Nietzsche also wants to deny this possibility as well. It is not clear whether or not Nietzsche believes that the denial of lack of overall change for any period of time implies the impossibility of lack of change in any particular thing for a period of time, but another note (WP 520), also from summer 1885, in which constant change is called 'continual transition', at least suggests that idea, while admitting that we do in fact perceive something like some degree of temporary lack of change within the world of becoming:

> Continual transition forbids us to speak of "individuals," etc; the "number" of beings is itself in flux. We would know nothing of time and motion if we did not, in a coarse fashion, believe we see what is at "rest" beside what is in motion. (KGW VII 36 [23])

The denial of "individuals" or "things", which is not quite the same thing as the denial of substances, I also will treat separately in the next chapter. But this passage, invoking as it does some principle of having to know something's "opposite" in order to know the thing itself, seems also to suggest that we do not come to know or believe that the world is in constant flux by simple observation of it. For such observation in fact gives us reason to believe that there is at least some temporary lack of change in some things for some durations. In that case, it would seem that the burden of proof should be on the one–in this case, Nietzsche–who maintains that everything is constantly changing, contrary to what I suggested above. But perhaps, as we shall see, that depends on what one might reasonably mean, and what Nietzsche means, by the idea of a "thing" constantly changing.

It is better, however, before we explore that idea, to mention another fundamental feature of Nietzsche's ontology that is relevant to the theory of constant change. That feature is his theory of *the will to power*. This theory, too, I will treat in more detail later, in the last chapter. But it is relevant in an important way to the theory of constant change, so something must be said about it here. Nietzsche's idea of the will to power is usually thought of in connection with human beings only or in particular, and then as involving a desire to dominate other people, especially through political power and even force. While it is true that Nietzsche usually spoke of the will to power in connection with the psychology of human beings, it is a misreading–a very serious misreading–of Nietzsche to suppose that it is to be understood, at least primarily, as the will to dominate others. On the contrary, with respect to human beings, the "purest" expression of the will to power is in self-domination, especially with self-improvement in connection with control of one's natural impulses in a way that allows for a productive harmony of reason and passion (in the 19th-century sense of, broadly, emotion). This is a large part of Nietzsche's idea of the *Übermensch* or "overman", the "higher type" of human being who excels, whether in the arts or the sciences or political life or otherwise.

But the will to power for Nietzsche is not a feature only of human or even of organic life. It is a completely general force in nature, one that is constantly, though not always or perhaps even usually successfully, acting on things (or "things") to become "better" members of their respective kinds, and to "expand" (in various senses) their places in nature. But my purpose here is not to try to explicate or recommend precisely what, if anything precise, this could reasonably mean, but to call attention to the claim of the constancy and the universality of this force. By 'constancy' I do not mean a sameness of the amount of force (whatever that could possibly mean in all the different ways in which the will to power is said by Nietzsche to be expressed) but only of existence: it is always there, in everything. And so being, the will to power is causing everything always to be striving, and so *changing*, to become a better member of its kind. Thus does the theory of the will to power support the theory of constant change; indeed, in its completely general form the theory of the will to power *entails* the theory of constant change, at least in some form or other. (John Richardson, too, connects the theory of constant change with the theory of the will to power, but in a somewhat different way, in an extensive and valuable discussion in his *Nietzsche's System*, 79-89.)

We know from physics that, in fact, everything is always changing, at least in the sense that there is always atomic motion going on in every bit of matter unless, what is never in fact the case apparently, that bit of matter is at a temperature of absolute zero. But this, obviously, is not quite what Nietzsche had in mind. And I think we must say here, as elsewhere, that probably Nietzsche really had nothing very precise in mind. But we can hope to give some precise formulations to what might be meant, in the context of Nietzsche's ontology, in saying that "all is in flux", not just in the sense that there is some change or other always taking place, but that every particular thing (or "thing") there is, is constantly changing.

Although it is all of a piece, we must to some extent distinguish the theory of constant change as applied to particular things from Nietzsche's rejection of substances and of "things". The theory operates at two levels, so to speak, with respect to particular things: first, in its rejection of an underlying substance in any such object, for example, a desk; and, second, in its affirmation of constant change of property or properties of the desk. The traditional ontological distinction of substance and property, in some form or other, is itself under attack, as we will see, by Nietzsche, but let us attend first to the idea of change of property, which, in some measure, we can consider independently, and which, in any case, is, if perhaps not more fundamental ontologically, of greater relevance to the thesis of constant change. If someone wants to maintain that any ordinary object is constantly changing in its properties, it would seem that he or she would need to affirm one of the following three possibilities:

(1) Every ordinary object, in any finite duration, changes at least one of its properties.

(2) Every ordinary object, in any finite duration, changes most of its properties.

(3) Every ordinary object, in any finite duration, changes all of its properties.

In order to assess any such thesis properly, we need to have, as Nietzsche did not, a precise, or at least somewhat more nearly precise, notion of property, and this in several respects. There is, first, the matter of distinguishing empirical from formal properties, categorical from dispositional properties, monadic from relational properties, and simple from complex properties. And, second, there is the matter of distinguishing among properties in their generality.

By an empirical property, we mean a property that either is given to one of the senses–a color, a texture, an odor, a taste, a sound–or that can be understood (that is, whose name can be defined) by way of such properties. So, for example, a particular shade of red is an empirical property. And even though, in a particular case, a formal property such as *being-a-particular* might be said to be given to, say, vision, such properties are not known in that way. And, of course, many other formal properties, such as *being-valid* (as applied to an argument) are not, even in that extended way, given to the senses. So let us say, although this is obviously not very useful in itself in the understanding of the notion, that a formal property is any property that is not an empirical property.

The property of *being-red* is a categorical property, that of *being-fragile* a dispositional property. This means, roughly, that we can tell that something is red just by looking at it, but that it is fragile only by running certain tests, so to speak. But *being-fragile* is an empirical property in that it can be understood by way of categorical empirical properties; in this case, the properties of *being-struck* and *breaking*. While there are various theories of exactly how the relevant definitions (the names of) of dispositional properties by way of (the names of) categorical properties should proceed (see Addis, 1981), we need not pursue this matter further, but simply agree that the dispositional properties of ordinary objects are a subset of their empirical properties.

Some properties an object can have in ontological independence (but not, of course, causal independence) of other objects, that is, even if it were the only object there is. So, for example, it is ontologically possible for the only thing to exist be an apple with its visual properties (even though, by hypothesis, there is no conscious being to look at it) of its color and its shape as well as its tactile and olfactory properties. Properties that an object has, or can have, in ontological independence of other objects, existing or not, are *monadic* properties. Properties that an object has, or can have, only in ontological dependence on other objects are *relational* properties. The *predicates* of natural languages very imperfectly match this distinction, especially insofar as some monadic predicates in fact refer to relational properties; for example, the predicate 'tall'. For a person cannot just be tall, so to speak, but only in relation to some other people. And we may take note of the obvious fact that if anything anywhere is moving at any given time (as is surely the case), then every object is changing its relational properties at that time: if the theory of constant change in its weakest form (change in at least one of its properties) is taken to apply to relational properties, therefore, it would unquestionably be true, at least as an empirical hypothesis, amounting to no more than the claim that at no time is the entire universe motionless.

The distinction between simple properties and complex properties is one that, according to many philosophers (possibly or even probably including Nietzsche, had he considered the issue), is not writ in nature itself but, if at all, only in a particular language or, possibly, way of thinking. Partly because I do not agree and partly because the possibility of its objective nature should be considered in any case with respect to the broader issue before us, I want very briefly to argue for the distinction as being in nature itself. The property of *being-(a particular shade of)-red* is a simple property; the property of *being-a-horse* is a complex property, or so I suggest. This means that the former has no constituents and cannot be understood (its name defined) by any such putative constituents. (It might be "defined" by way of definite descriptions such as one specifying its location on the spectrum and, of course, partly defined by its "genus", the property of *being-a-color*.) But the property of *being-a-horse* obviously does have constituents, and (the names of) these properties–for example, that of *having-two-ears*–may well enter the definition of that property. As should be evident, the dispute is not whether or not there are any such complex properties but whether or not there are any genuinely simple properties. And my example is meant to suggest an affirmative answer to the latter. And in discussing the possible exact meanings of the thesis that every ordinary object is constantly changing its properties, I will assume the truth of that answer.

As the redness of a leaf darkens in the fall, we say naturally that it is changing color, even though it remains red. If we think of this in the old language of genus/species (although, of course, there are more than two levels in almost any context in which that distinction might be applied), we would say that while the genus has remained the same, the species of it has changed. And at the next level "up" we would say that of something that has changed from red to blue that, while it has remained colored, it has changed its color. None of this goes very deep ontologically, but we must also keep these matters in mind in specifying and evaluating any thesis about constant change of property.

The first thing to be said about Nietzsche's theory that every ordinary object is constantly undergoing change of property (one, most, or all) is that the domain of properties at issue is certainly that, and that only, of empirical properties, just as the effect of the will to power on individual things, including human beings, has to do exclusively with empirical properties. One might, to be very careful, say that, if ordinary objects have any formal properties, then any change in them will be contingent on changes in their empirical properties; there could not be any change of the formal properties of an object without change in its empirical properties. So we may restrict our discussion entirely to change of empirical properties. And let us here remind ourselves that we understand an empirical property to be one that either is given to one or more of the senses of that can be understood (its name defined) by means of such properties.

Thus, we are talking about the ordinary properties of ordinary objects, just the kinds of properties that a person would be likely to mention if asked to describe such an object or a person. Especially in the case of persons, such descriptions are likely to include dispositional as well as categorical properties, but we may here take note of the fact that nothing can change its dispositional properties without changing some of its categorical properties. The details of this idea are complex, but the general idea is that if, as is the case on all theories of the nature of dispositional properties, such properties are to be understood in whole or in part by way of categorical properties, there would be no ontological basis for, or epistemological access to, dispositional properties otherwise. So now, safely ignoring the fact that the categorical properties of an object may change without its changing its dispositional properties, we may say that we can restrict the discussion of the thesis of constant change of properties to categorical, empirical properties.

So, finally, let us consider some ordinary object–an apple sitting on a table before us and given to sight, for example–and ask how the theory of constant change, understood as the theory that at least one, or most, or all of the categorical, empirical properties of an object change in any finite duration, fares. Are any of these the case with respect to the apple?

We saw above, in a quote from Nietzsche, his apparent agreement that we believe that some of what we see is "at rest". But keeping in mind that he uses his thesis of constant change to attack the notion that there really are things at all, that is, distinct individual objects, we cannot suppose, as we might be initially tempted, that the thesis is only that objects are constantly in motion; that would be no reason at all to deny that there are things or substances. (As already promised, this language of things and substances, and the ideas and confusions inherent in Nietzsche's use it, will be sorted out in the next chapter.) So we must continue to assume that the thesis applies not only to the "dynamic" properties of objects but equally to their other properties.

The apple, as we gaze upon it, appears at least for some time not to change any of its categorical, empirical properties at all. We know, of course, that it changes its relational properties if, for example, anything else anywhere moves; and knowing that, we know therefore that everything constantly changes its relational properties. And we know from physics that the apple is constantly changing in the properties of the atoms and molecules of which it is constituted. But these changes again seem uninteresting and irrelevant with respect to what we must assume to be Nietzsche's theory. (But we can imagine that, even though he was a critic of atomic theory, Nietzsche would be somehow pleased with the fact of constant change at the atomic level.)

I think we have to insist that the evidence of our senses very strongly suggests the falsity of Nietzsche's theory, even in its weakest form–that at least one property of every ordinary object, for any finite duration, changes. Nietzsche was, or at least eventually became, very much a philosophical friend of the senses, keeping in mind the passage from *Twilight of the Idols* in praise of Heraclitus quoted above, as well as these words that follow soon after:

> And what magnificent instruments of observation we possess in our senses! This nose, for example, of which no philosopher has yet spoken with reverence and gratitude, is actually the most delicate instrument so far at our disposal: it is able to detect minimal differences of motion which even a spectroscope cannot detect. (TI "'Reason' in Philosophy" 3)

But let us also keep in mind the sentences in that earlier passage that read "Heraclitus too did the senses an injustice. They lie neither in the way the Eleactics believed, nor as he believed–they do not lie at all. What we make of their testimony, that alone introduces lies..." These passages together suggest two possible ways for Nietzsche to reject the claim above about the evidence of our senses with respect to the theory of constant change.

The first reply that Nietzsche might make is to insist that we are not being careful enough in our attention to the evidence of our senses, that if we attend more carefully to the visual data in looking at the apple, we will, after all, be able to detect constant change in the apple. It is perhaps curious that Nietzsche speaks, in his tribute to the nose, of change of *motion*, as if, possibly, that were, after all, the kind of change the theory is about. Nor is it clear that the sense of smell has a lot to do with detecting changes of motion. But as to the suggestion itself: each will have to speak for him- or herself, I suppose; but as for me: attend as closely as I can, I cannot discern any change in my relevant visual data as I gaze upon the apple. I am no enemy of the real possibility that there are features of my visual data that are escaping my attention, but in the case at hand, the onus would appear to be on the one–Nietzsche, in this case–who insists that there are such data, whether or not I have succeeded in becoming aware of them.

The other reply is for Nietzsche to agree that we not only do not but, through however careful attention, cannot detect the relevant changes by looking at the apple, but that we know on independent grounds that at least one, most, or all of the properties we are aware of are in fact changing. But with this we are back to the idea of the will to power or some other, as yet unmentioned reason for believing in the theory of constant change. And, of course, then the theory of the will to power, or that other reason, would itself need defense.

Perhaps Nietzsche would be content to rest his theory of constant change on the theory of the will to power. That gives it, I would judge, a weak and ill-defined basis, insofar as the theory of the will to power is itself an amorphous and very poorly defended theory–in Nietzsche's or anyone else's hands. I intend to say more about it later, but say here that I regard it as the least defensible aspect of Nietzsche's ontology. Its main problem, perhaps, is its vagueness; and while the theory of eternal return is probably at least as improbable–which is very highly improbable--as the theory of the will to power, at least it has a relatively clear meaning.

The theory of constant change, then, in the sense that I have argued that Nietzsche meant it, seems to me to be false: it is not the case that even at least one empirical, categorical property of every object, for every finite duration, changes. Every ordinary object changes constantly, to be sure, and maybe in the end Nietzsche would be satisfied with that, if he could bring himself, after all, to accept some version of atomic theory.

But I think that what is really going on in the end, as at least the tone of the long quote about the "philosophers" from *Twilight of the Idols* suggests, is that Nietzsche feels he must make an absolute distinction between the world of being and the world of becoming–so thorough as to encompass the theory of constant change. He cannot abide the idea that anything in the natural world–the only world on his (and my) view–has even a degree of permanence. To do so would be to make a dangerous concession to the "philosophers" who, according to Nietzsche, cannot themselves abide the idea of becoming.

All of this will become clearer if we now turn to Nietzsche's attack on the theory of substance and "things", an ontologically more profound topic than that of constant change.

SUBSTANCES AND THINGS

Although Nietzsche's rejection of substances and "things" (or "thinghood") is well-known and moderately well-discussed, it is not easy to get into this matter in detail. The reason is, if I am not mistaken, that he is the victim–not the first or the last–of a fundamental confusion in failing adequately to distinguish the realm of the ontological from that of common sense and its "long arm" science, as Bergmann calls it (1964, 337). This I hope to demonstrate in the pages that follow. But I propose to begin with an historical and systematic review of the ontological notion of substance.

We must be clear at the outset that, in speaking of substance as the philosophers do, we are speaking of something that has nothing to do with that other, most important meaning of the term–that of the chemists (American sense), in which the identity of a substance is specified by its atomic or molecular constitution. And although Nietzsche rejected atomic theory (for not very good reasons), he surely had, or would have had, no problem with the idea that, at a certain level, things can be distinguished as to whether they are oxygen or hydrogen or sodium, and so on, however those distinctions are to be made. No, Nietzsche was clear, as we must be, that the questions of the nature and existence of substance, as they concern the philosopher, and more specifically the ontologist, are of quite a different order. Hereafter, in speaking of substance, I will be referring exclusively to the philosophical notion of it.

In the tradition of Western philosophy, the notion of substance operates at different ontological levels, and even has somewhat different meanings. Without trying to specify them, we may say that, for the purposes at hand–those of discussing Nietzsche's rejection of substance–we are dealing entirely with the notion of an *individual substance*, the sense in which, according to those philosophers who believe in substance, every ordinary object is said to be a substance. Thus a carrot is a substance, a star is a substance, and a human being is a substance. In the case of human beings, and possibly some other objects, there is a complication insofar as some philosophers, most notably René Descartes, held that a human being, at least in this world, is some kind of combination or "unity" of *two* substances, one physical and one mental. And in the chapter on Nietzsche's views on the nature of the mind, I shall want to discuss this "complication". Here, though, we may ignore it, and proceed on the assumption that, on the theory in question, every ordinary object is *a* substance

We may also, for the purposes at close hand but not for the broader topic of this chapter, ignore the question of what exactly counts as an ordinary object. For Nietzsche's attack on substance is intended to apply, and does apply, to the paradigm examples of the tradition; if it is successful there, it will obviously apply–even more so, one might say–to "things" like the "object" composed exhaustively of my left hand and the great galaxy in Andromeda. If a carrot isn't a substance, then nothing is a substance.

What, then, is an individual substance? Or, more precisely put, what features has the Western philosophical tradition ascribed to the notion of such a substance, leaving open the question whether or not anything actually has some or all of those features? Keeping in mind that they are not all of equal importance, either in themselves or in the tradition or in the context of Nietzsche's critique of substance, we may identify the following six features: A substance is said to be (1) *an ultimate subject of properties,* (2) *independent,* (3) *natured,* (4) *active,* (5) *unanalyzable,* and (6) *a continuant.* The last of these features is the most important for our purposes, but let us first say something about each of the others.

In saying that a substance is an ultimate subject of properties, one means that a substance is a subject of properties but is not itself the property of anything. Some things *may* be both a subject of a property and the property of something else; for example, the property of *being-red* might be said to be both a property of certain substances but also a subject of the property of *being-a-color.* The thesis of elementarism denies that there are any properties of properties, holding in the example at hand that, on ontological analysis, color should be treated, like red itself, as a "first-level" property of individual things: whatever is red is colored. And, too, some philosophers have held an ontology according to which ordinary objects, whether or not they are identified as substances, are themselves properties of something else. Spinoza is a possible example, maybe even Descartes, and, among more recent philosophers, C. I. Lewis, all of whom might be read as saying that individual things are properties of a god or of the world as a whole. But the standard view of substance ontologists has been that an ordinary object, in being or having as a constituent a substance, is an ultimate subject of properties.

In being an ultimate subject of properties, an individual substance is also said to be independent. That is, while properties depend for their existence on substances, substances can exist alone. It is not, of course, *causal* independence that is at issue here, for it is obvious and uncontroversial that every ordinary object is causally dependent for its existence on other objects. I think it is false or at least misleading to say, as Aristotle and others following did say, that, to quote Aristotle, "Now there are several senses in which a thing is said to be first; yet substance is first in every sense – (1) in definition, (2) in order of knowledge, (3) in time. For (3) of the other categories none can exist independently, but only substance." (1941, 783) My reason is, as I argued in a paper on Aristotle on the independence of substances (1972) that, just as a property cannot exist without being exemplified (here I am with Aristotle against Plato), so a substance (or an ordinary object, whether or not it is, strictly speaking, a substance) cannot exist without exemplifying properties. But we can appreciate the rough idea that ordinary objects, considered as particular things exemplifying certain properties, have ontological independence, which is another way of saying that a universe consisting of just one ordinary object is ontologically possible.

To be natured, as applied at least to particular things, is to have some property more intimately than others, that property being its nature or its essence or its form, as the tradition speaks. (Aristotle, and some others, also call this special property a secondary substance.) The nature of a carrot, for example, is the essence or property of its being a carrot, whereas its other properties that are not part of its essence–its particular length, for example–are said to be its accidents. Thus a substance is sometimes said, ontologically speaking, to be a unity of matter (but not in the physicists' sense) and of form; and it is this entity that exemplifies accidents. One can hold a substance ontology in all the other respects without being bound to the thesis that there are essential properties; but most substance philosophers have affirmed some kind of distinction between essential properties and other properties.

The notion of activity, in Western philosophy, is perhaps inherently vague, but it is connected, in some cases, with that of free will in humans or so-called "agent" causation. The rough idea is that a substance is a primary source of change, whereas other entities, such as properties, are not. But it is partly this feature of substance that led some philosophers to doubt or deny that ordinary objects, including human beings, really are substances insofar as this would seem to imply that there are, in addition to God, other fundamental sources of change and motion. Spinoza, even though his god is not (I say) a conscious being, is clear in denying that "finite modes" (that is, ordinary objects) are substances. And even Descartes leans toward saying that his god, that of Christianity, is the only substance, strictly speaking, even though he is also famously known for his two-substance theory of human beings. Although, as we know and will see in detail shortly, Nietzsche is a vehement opponent of substance philosophy, he may, on this matter, be said to be not entirely unsympathetic, given his theory of the will to power. For that theory very much suggests that in every individual thing, there is an inherent capacity for initiating and continuing change and motion. At the same time, as we will also see in greater detail later, his critique of substance relies in part on the claim that the origin of the idea lies in an indefensible notion of the self as a "doer", that is, as an independent source of change. But, perhaps needless to say, this philosophical notion of activity as a feature of substances has long since been rejected by most philosophers, especially those most influenced by developments in science, and specifically the law of inertial motion, coming from Galileo and Newton. The contemporary scientific worldview has no place for any such notion.

Even though much of the tradition of substance ontology has held that an individual substance is "made up" of matter and form, it was also usually held that the substance is simple in the sense of being unanalyzable. This could mean, and for some probably did mean, something like the idea that neither matter nor form is capable of independent existence, or even the related, but more radical, idea that neither is an existent–that the simplest existent is a combination, a unity of matter and form (see Veatch, 1974).

But there is another, more important sense in which substances are not analyzable and which leads us to the critical idea of a substance as a continuant. For it is fundamental to substance ontology that a substance not be analyzable into temporal "parts" (spatial parts do not seem to be a worry, or at least not as much of a worry): a substance does not consist, in the ontological sense, of momentary particulars that are temporally contiguous to each other or of "time slices". But we must examine this notion of a substance as a continuant more carefully.

In the ordinary sense, an entity is a continuant if it persists through time. By this simple measure, a desk is a continuant, a rainbow is a continuant, a person is a continuant, the universe itself is a continuant. Does that mean than any or all of them are also substances? One can, of course, use the word 'substance' so that any continuant is a substance, but we must cut things finer in order not to give a trivial, affirmative answer to the question. That we have already begun to do in saying that a substance is not analyzable into temporal "parts". It must be *simple*, not just in the sense of not having further constituents at a moment, but also in the sense of not consisting of a series of momentary particulars. It must be literally the same simple entity from the beginning to the end of its existence. It is in this much stronger sense that it is controversial and interesting whether or not there are substances. Let us mark this distinction between the controversial and the trivial notions of continuant by distinguishing *ontological continuants* from *commonsense continuants*. An ontological continuant is a simple, enduring particular while a commonsense continuant is any particular, simple or not, that endures. So, necessarily, an ontological continuant is also a commonsense continuant.

(The distinction, as made, between ontological and commonsense continuants applies, obviously, only to those entities that are in time. As we know, philosophical theists almost invariably hold that a god is a substance. And most of them hold also that such a god is not in time. Thus, the notion of being a continuant would not apply. Still, the notion of simplicity is very much still thought to be relevant. All, or nearly all, such philosophers hold that a god is a simple entity, at least in the sense that it is ontologically impossible for it to "break up" into yet simpler entities. And it does have all of the other features of substance I listed above, most notably, independence and being active, even though the latter would seem also to require time.)

But a further distinction will be worth our while here with respect to commonsense continuants. More precisely, we want to ask what would make something *a* commonsense continuant, ontologically speaking, if it is not also an ontological continuant. Of course, for those who believe that all ordinary objects are ontological continuants–that is, substances–this question does not arise except, in a somewhat different form, as an epistemological one. Still, in light of what is to come with respect to Nietzsche's attack on the theories of substance and "things", it will be important to see how a philosopher who believes in commonsense but not ontological continuants might answer the question.

We will capture the notion of commonsense continuant adequately for most purposes if we say that to be a commonsense continuant is for an ordinary object to have the so-called "orbit" feature. Consider Descartes' ball of wax in the *Meditations.* Even through rapid change of properties, either it remains in roughly the same place relative to other nearby objects or, if it does move relative to the objects, it occupies all the spaces in between by whatever route it takes. How else would we know, if we could not observe these features, that it is the same ball of wax through time? Descartes took it for granted that it was the same object through time, and was more interested in establishing the role of the mind in the understanding of what it is to be an object; but the example, extreme as it is, makes clear what is meant by the orbit feature. In the absence of observation of the orbit feature, which is not the basis for most of our ascriptions of sameness of object through time, we necessarily rely on observation or knowledge of sameness or similarity of properties ultimately as well as assumptions of lawful regularity in our judgments of sameness of objects through time. It is because minds can never be observed to have the orbit feature that one can reasonably doubt not only that a mind is an ontological continuant but even that it is a commonsense continuant (see Addis, 1989, 151-161). For, unless a mind is, after all, an ontological continuant, then in dreamless sleep or when a person is otherwise unconscious, the mind does not exist. Thus minds, on this view, have an even weaker degree of cohesion of a sort that makes them only what we may call *intentional-perspectival* continuants. But the ontology of mind, and Nietzsche's views of it, we will discuss later. Let us now, restricting ourselves to ordinary physical objects, say that they are either ontological continuants or else merely commonsense continuants.

Nietzsche tells us that there are no substances, but also that there are no "things". I put 'things' in double quotes because (1) the word is such a general term that it applies to everything (it is not easy to speak non-tautologically at this level, so to speak), and Nietzsche, like everyone else, often uses the word–singular or plural–casually and without ontological commitment; and (2) Nietzsche's use of the word hovers, sometimes in the same passage, between a mere (!) rejection of substance ontology and a much more radical rejection of anything whatsoever in reality itself that could provide an ontological ground for sameness through time. In any case, I want now to suggest that it will be useful, if not wholly accurate, to map my relatively precise notions of *ontological continuant* and *commonsense continuant* onto Nietzsche's notions of *substance* and *thing*, respectively, which leaves us with the thesis that there are no continuants at all, either ontological or commonsensical. But the matter is not quite that simple, as we shall see.

It will be further useful if, before detailed discussion of these matters, I set out Nietzsche's primary theses with respect to the issues before us, although, as just indicated, we shall have to cut things much finer than he did in order to evaluate these and related theses. Here, then, are what I take to be the crucial claims that Nietzsche makes with respect to substances and "things":

(1) There are no substances, that is, ontological continuants do not exist.

(2) The primary source of the notion of substance lies in the idea of the self as a "doer".

(3) The idea of the self as a "doer" is indefensible.

(4) There are no "things", that is, commonsense continuants do not exist.

(5) The belief in, or at least the assumption of, ordinary objects as continuants–ontological or commonsensical–is necessary to everyday existence.

(6) The independent truth of formal logic, including the law of non-contradiction, rests on the assumption that there are continuants.

(7) Because there are no continuants, formal logic is only a projection by us onto the world, not an independent set of truths about reality.

(8) An ordinary object is only a "bundle" of its properties.

(9) "Bundles" of properties do not qualify as "things".

We may take the first three of these as expressing Nietzsche's rejection of substance in particular, the next four his broader attack on the idea of reality as structured in a way that allows for things to an extent that would ground the applicability of formal logic, and the last two his "positive" theory as to how the world is with respect to ordinary objects. I will contend, as we continue, that Nietzsche is right to reject substance ontology but that his reasons are highly questionable, that he is wrong to reject commonsense continuants and the independent basis of formal logic, and that he is probably wrong to embrace bundle theory, but that even the bundle theory would be sufficient to affirm commonsense continuants and the independent basis of formal logic.

But I begin with a fundamental point regarding the connection between the theory of constant change and the denial of the existence of continuants–ontological or commonsensical. And the point will be most forcefully made if we restrict ourselves to substance. That point is that *the theory of constant change, at least with respect to change of properties, does not entail a denial of the existence of substances.* For, whether we take constant change to be, for any finite duration, change of at least one property, change of most properties, or even change of all properties of an ordinary object, then, if substances are possible at all, such an object could be (or, if you prefer, have as a constituent) a substance. And this is so whether change of property be taken either qualitatively or quantitatively or even as the coming into or going out of existence of the particular exemplification of the property. But there is an important qualification: a substance cannot lose its essential property and remain the substance it is. In that sense, a given substance cannot really change all of its properties. If "it" changes "its" essential property, "it" becomes a different *kind* of substance and hence a different substance. So "it" is not an it, but a they.

As we know, one of the basic feature of the notion of an individual substance is that of ultimate subject of properties (or "substratum", as some would speak, but this notion has undesirable epistemological connotations), that is, of what remains the same through change of property. Its essential property, its nature, does not change, but its "accidents"–the properties, or values of properties, that are not essential to its being the kind of thing it is–ordinarily will change, if not necessarily during any finite duration, at least at some time in the existence of the object.

Did Nietzsche believe otherwise? Was he unaware that one of the primary motivations and arguments in the history of the theory of substance was to account, ontologically, for sameness through change? Surely not. And yet he repeatedly contrasts the "permanence" of substance with the facts of becoming and change, as if the theory of substance entailed a realm of "eternal" objects whose existence would be inconsistent with the theory of constant change. Perhaps then we must go deeper, keeping in mind Nietzsche's rejection of atomism, by setting out the various ontological possibilities with respect to *particularity* before we ask further just what Nietzsche's view *might* have been had it been given precise formulation, and whether or not his denial of things as well as substances is really demanded by his theory of constant change.

An ordinary object, whether it be a physical object such as a carrot, or a mental object such as a fleeting thought of what one is having for supper or even a mind itself, is something either in both space and time or, in the case of mental objects, perhaps only in time. While every ordinary object is a *particular* thing, it also has features that are shared with other ordinary objects; namely, its properties. This problem of how an object can be both one thing and yet have features shared with other objects we know as that of the One and the Many. It is the One, so to speak, that is our present concern–what it is about an ordinary object, on ontological analysis, that is or grounds its oneness, its particularity. In the Western philosophical tradition, there are, on the most general level, three major possibilities in accounting for the particularity of ordinary objects:

> (1) The particularity of an ordinary object is grounded in its being or containing a *substance*, that is, an ontological continuant that is an entity that is different in ontological category from properties. (This is the traditional substance view, which we have already discussed at some length.)

> (2) The particularity of an ordinary object is grounded in the *momentary particulars* that are among its constituents and that are dif-

ferent in ontological category from properties. The object is comprised of such particulars exemplifying certain properties and standing in certain spatial, temporal, and lawful relations to each other. (This is a view that comes out of the analytic, phenomenalist tradition.)

(3) The particularity of an ordinary object is grounded in the fact that its properties constitute a *bundle*, that is, stand in some relation or relations to each other of a sort that make(s) them the properties of the same ordinary object. On this theory, unlike the other two, there are no *simple* particulars different in ontological category from properties. (This is also a view that comes out of the analytic, phenomenalist tradition.)

Some philosophers, especially but by no means only those trained in the Thomist tradition, would no doubt describe the theories of either the second or the third possibilities as denying that there are any "real" things at all. Things, for these philosophers, have no "substantial unity", nothing at all that persists through the existence of the ordinary object and that is peculiar to that object, unless such objects are substances. And in the case of the mind, which we will turn to separately in the next chapter, these same philosophers are likely to insist that, if minds are not substances, then there is no such thing as the self. For on both of these ontologies that deny the existence of substances, whatever is peculiar to the ordinary object–the momentary particulars of the second possibility–do not persist through the existence of the ordinary object, while what does persist of the third possibility–the bundling relation(s)–are not peculiar to it (or else–a sub-possibility that we may ignore–such a relation is structurally a simple particular, indeed a substance after all). And the properties themselves are, by assumption, non-persisting and non-peculiar unless they are so-called "perfect particulars" or tropes, that is, particular to the object that has it, in which case, if they are also said to be in space and time, are structurally individual and, indeed, effectively natured substances in themselves.

I want now to suggest that Nietzsche is the "mirror image" of those substance philosophers who say, in effect, that if there are no substances, then there are no things. They complete their reasoning by *modus tollens* ("There are things. So, there are substances") while Nietzsche insists on the corresponding *modus ponens* ("There are no substances. So, there are no things"). The substance philosophers take the argument as a *reductio ad absurdum* that proves the existence of substances, Nietzsche a counter-*reductio* that demonstrates the non-existence of things. And as to Nietzsche's views on this matter, I cannot find any controversy or even much discussion in the literature.

Both Nietzsche and the substance philosophers are mistaken, as I shall shortly argue, in accepting the conditional ("If there are no substances, then there are no things") to begin with. But, in Nietzsche's case, this is to say, in effect, that he conflated substances and things, that is, what I call ontological continuants and commonsense continuants. For the implication in the other direction–if there are no things (commonsense continuants), then there are no substances (ontological continuants)–no one would dispute, not *even* Nietzsche, perhaps one should add! But before we look at Nietzsche's other arguments against substances, let us consider the issue in itself in a few paragraphs.

There are, I believe, decisive reasons for rejecting the idea of a simple constituent of an ordinary object that endures through time and change of the properties it exemplifies, even though, as we noted earlier, one of the "defining" features of the idea is that of what remains the same through change, as "substratum" and that in which the succession of properties or of different values of the same property inhere. But the fact of change, even of constant change however specified, does not, *contra* Nietzsche, entail that there are no substances.

At the same time, there is an important connection between the notion of substance and that of time that does cast severe doubt on the substance ontology. In brief, the argument is that the only way to avoid violation of the law of non-contradiction with an ontology of substance is to combine that ontology with one of absolute time, that is, an ontology according to which there are ordered *moments* that exist as simple entities independent of ordinary objects. So instead of having the simplest relevant facts being, for example, that *the leaf is green* and *the leaf is not green* which, by themselves, are contradictory, one has *the leaf is green at t1* and *the leaf is not green at t2*. This seems fairly obvious, but insofar as it is supposed to be ontologically relevant, it commits its proponent to absolute time. But, at least if one is broadly empiricist, the theory of absolute time is itself probably false: we are not acquainted in our experience with anything reasonably called moments, but instead "construct" the idea of moments from temporal relations, which themselves hold between and among ordinary objects and events or at least some of their constituents. This, of course, is only a very brief sketch of an argument that can be made in detail (see Bergmann, 1959a, 230-231), but it indicates one fundamental if somewhat technical reason why some philosophers of the empiricist, analytic tradition reject substance ontology.

But the broader empiricist tradition has rejected substance ontology, though not always completely, for somewhat different reasons, some of which are also Nietzsche's. These tend to be more epistemological in character, roughly, that we are not *acquainted* with any substance as such in our experience. (George Berkeley, a somewhat special case among major philosophers, rejected *material* substances on the ground that *activity* can pertain only to mental things.) Invoking the feature of substance as *substratum,* the empiricists were skeptical of anything that is hidden from experience. David Hume's ontology is the eventual culmination of this line of thought, in which there are neither material nor mental substances; and Nietzsche's views are not much different.

For Nietzsche, the idea that there are substances but with which we are not acquainted in ordinary experience (meaning sense experience and introspection) would introduce, or reintroduce as it did in Immanuel Kant's philosophy, the ontologically and morally suspect two-worlds idea of "higher" and "lower" strata. Whether it takes the form of Plato's distinction between an eternal world of "being"–the world of forms–and an inferior "copy" of that world in the realm of "becoming"; or the Christian's distinction between this everyday, created world with beginning and end and another, eternal world inhabited by necessarily bodiless beings (even if we humans are said to be able to exist in both worlds); or Kant's distinction between "mere" phenomena and the "real" world of things-in-themselves including selves-in-themselves, any such distinction is, for Nietzsche, absurd-in-itself and reveals a contemptible depreciation of the world of everyday life and experience. In particular, Nietzsche claims to see a hatred of the body and sexuality, of birth and death, of change itself, and a refusal to face the reality that this everyday world is the only world there is.

But we need not follow Nietzsche in his analysis (or, rather, speculations) of the psychological sources of the belief in one or another form of a two-worlds view in order to appreciate his post-Kantian, and still plausible, objection to substances along empiricist lines. Perhaps, finally to introduce a text from Nietzsche on the issue, his clearest, if somewhat succinct, statement of this argument appears in a note of 1886-87 (WP 553):

> The sore spot of Kant's critical philosophy has gradually become visible even to dull eyes: Kant no longer has a right to his distinction "appearance" and "thing-in-itself"–he had deprived himself of the right to go on distinguishing in this old familiar way, in so far as he rejected as impermissible making inferences from phenomena to a cause of phenomena–in accordance with his conception of causality and its purely intra-phenomenal validity–which conception, on the other hand, already anticipates this distinction, as if the "thing-in-itself" were not only inferred but *given*. (KGW VIII 5 [4], Nietzsche's emphasis)

Here, to be sure, Nietzsche's explicit point is to locate an internal inconsistency in Kant's philosophy, but the tone, if no more, makes apparent Nietzsche's hostility to the "thing-in-itself" as well as the epistemological ground of that hostility. It may be useful to add here that Nietzsche does himself reject the doctrine of the given, in the strict sense, as we shall see in discussion of his ontology of mind; but this is combined, in something of a Berkeleyan manner, that is, a *phenomenalist* manner, with a rejection of any ontological distinction between appearance and reality. With Berkeley, Nietzsche would say (and I would emphatically agree) that, while of course we are sometimes mistaken in our perceptions or what we make of them, we should never be tempted to conclude from that fact that there is some kind of non-perceptual reality "behind" or "beyond" or "beneath" what we can see that is the way things really are as contrasted with the way they appear. One can make a local distinction between, for example, how this apple appears in this poor light and how it really is, as seen in full sunlight; but that is a long way from a cosmic distinction between appearance and reality in which we have direct access only to appearance and never to reality.

Having introduced the idea of phenomenalism, I must stress that it is the phenomenalism of the early analytic tradition as represented by Bertrand Russell and A. J. Ayer and the Vienna Circle, though stretching back to John Stuart Mill and Ernst Mach, of which I am speaking, a notion I believe will be helpful to us in understanding Nietzsche's views. So understood, we may also say that phenomenalism hovered uncertainly between idealism, a philosophy all of these philosophers were emphatic in rejecting explicitly, according to which physical objects are composed wholly of "sense data" where such data are thought of as actually existing only when someone "has" them, and a theory, while explicitly rejecting any metaphysical pretensions, according to which every meaningful statement, except for those of logic and mathematics, could be "translated into" or "rewritten as" or otherwise "correlated with" a statement that mentions only simple entities of actual or possible experience. John Stuart Mill, for example, in a memorable phrase wrote of "the permanent possibilities of sensation".

But *ontologically*, and whether or not some or all of its constituents are held to mind-independent (many of these philosophers, especially the logical positivists, holding such a matter to be "meaningless" metaphysics), a physical object is, on this way of thinking, some kind of complex of momentary and other simple entities all of which are, or could be, objects of sense experience. It is this last idea, and indeed a particular version of it, that is even more to the point with regard to Nietzsche's rejection of substances (and therefore "things"), and that I wish to invoke in connection with his second important reason or argument against substances. This argument is stated in a note of 1887 (WP 558), as follows:

> The "thing-in-itself" nonsensical. If I remove all the relationships, all the "properties," all the "activities" of a thing, the thing does not remain over; because thingness has only been invented by us owing to the requirements of logic, thus with the aim of defining, communication (to bind together the multiplicity of relationships, properties, activities). (KGW VIII 10 [202])

Here we have something of what I suppose we might identify as an argument from ontological economy–the use of the principle of Occam's Razor–although there is also mention of a further thesis in his mention of "the requirements of logic" which I will discuss separately. As for the argument from ontological economy, I restate it as follows: an ordinary object can be analyzed, ontologically, as consisting only of properties and relations (under which I subsume "activities"); there is no need for an entity or entities from an additional category of particular or individual– whether momentary or enduring–to be the subject of those properties and relations. In short, there are no *simple* particulars–at least there is no good reason to suppose that there are–and an ordinary object, which is, in the present context, a *complex* particular thing, consists only of a *bundle* of its properties and relations.

So I am now suggesting, tentatively, that it is reasonable to ascribe to Nietzsche the third of the major possibilities that I identified earlier, the bundle theory. (The second theory, which has momentary particulars as well as properties and relations among its categories of simple entities is also sometimes called a bundle theory, probably most often by its critics of the substance tradition.) And I have suggested also that his most immediate intellectual reason for holding this theory is the principle of ontological economy. But it must be said that there is little other than the passage I cited in Nietzsche's writings that directly supports this view, although I shall soon cite other passages that are less directly relevant to it. And in any case, whether or not the view is defensible, one might further suggest that here Nietzsche is a victim, if that is the right word, of that common defect he so often and sometimes brilliantly identifies in others–coming to a certain view because of one's *values* and only subsequently finding, or imagining oneself to have found, an intellectual basis for it. But this idea, in turn, which Nietzsche thought to be shocking to his readers and which is now overindulged in by contemporary postmodernists and others, should cause little more than a shrug of the shoulders in us who clearly recognize the distinction between the causal origins of a theory–whether in general at the social level or in the individual at the psychological level–on the one hand, and the reasons that can be given for its truth or plausibility on the other. This distinction, essential for thinking rationally about the history of ideas (and much else besides), I discussed in an earlier chapter.

So, here ignoring altogether what values pushed Nietzsche toward the bundle theory, let us briefly evaluate the theory itself. Let us consider a simple example in which, for the purpose at hand, we can ignore change. A red, round spot, on the bundle theory, will consist at least of the properties of red and round. But no serious ontologist could leave it at that. For the mere *set* of those properties can hardly be a particular thing. Thus there must be something else that somehow binds red and round together in this case to make this a particular red spot. The usual answer is that there is, in addition to red and round and whatever ordinary relations one might want to include as constituents of the spot, a special relation that *binds* together those properties and ordinary relations to make a particular object. And this answer, however yet vague, may seem adequate, even if it is, in a sense, saying that a particular object is more than a mere bundle of properties.

But if we modify our example by adding a second red spot beside the first, we encounter a more serious problem. One principle of general ontology–perhaps the most important–is that two objects, be they physical objects or mental objects, cannot have all of their constituents in common. Otherwise, there is no account of their being two and not one. So, it would seem that each of our two red, round spots cannot consist only of red, round, and the binding relation, *if* each of these entities is a universal, that is, that each of those simple entities is literally the same entity in both spots. One apparent solution to this problem, and one that some philosophers have advocated, is to invoke the unique spatial/temporal location of each individual thing. The usual reply to this suggestion is that the particularity and, in the case at hand, the twoness of the spots is ontologically prior to their spatial/temporal locations and cannot be secured by those locations. This is another way of saying that space and time, whatever they are exactly themselves, are not *constituents* of ordinary objects while the particularity and uniqueness of an object is somehow grounded in its constituents.

The only other solution to this dilemma would seem to be to affirm that not all, and maybe none, of the entities countenanced by the bundle theory are universals; that either properties and ordinary relations are particular to the objects that have them (are *tropes*, in contemporary jargon), or that the binding relation at least is particular to the object that has it, or that all these entities are particular to the objects that have them. But if, in order to account for the two spots both being red, one holds that only the binding relation is particular, one is, in effect, back to a view of particulars and universals that is more like the second major theory. And a curious theory it is, with some relations being universals and one being particular to its objects. It would surely be better, then, to adopt the second theory itself, as originally stated, on which the distinction between particulars one the one hand and properties and relations on the other is sharply drawn.

This is probably the best place to consider Hales's and Welshon's extended discussion of bundle theories (as promised in the first chapter) which they do in the context of what they call Nietzsche's "perspectivist ontology of power." Valuable as their discussion is, it relies on, if I am not mistaken, some serious confusions, which confusions call into question the plausibility of their interpretation of Nietzsche's views on the nature of "things", although some of the confusion, if that is what it is, may well be found in Nietzsche himself. But let us begin with their notion of a "perspectivist" ontology.

In their book, the notion of such an ontology is, to my eyes, nowhere precisely stated, but in a collection of essays on Nietzsche and the sciences (1999, 41), Welshon puts the idea as follows:

> According to Nietzsche, perspectives are mapped to both quanta of power and societies of power. So, each atomic quantum event and every molecular society of events generates a perspective. Nietzsche affirms that there is an interpretation or perspective for every quantum of power and for every level of complexity above the fundamental level as well. Thus, where there are distinct societies of force, there too are distinct interpretations on the balance. Since there is an infinity of quanta and societies of power, there is an infinity of perspectives, as claimed in *The Gay Science*, section 374.

Welshon also refers his readers to entries 259, 567, 637, and 639 of *The Will to Power* and entry 34 of *Beyond Good and Evil* in support of what he says. I refer my readers to the same passages with the suggestion that in the two of them, GS 374 and WP 567, that might even seem to support the idea of a "perspectivist" ontology, it is not at all clear that Nietzsche is writing of "centers of force" beyond the human or perhaps the animal realm, that is, where conscious beings are involved and where, therefore we can talk about perspectives in a minimally intelligible sense. And in WP637, he even tells us that the idea of an atom of force's being "concerned only with its own neighborhood" because "distant forces balance one another"–surely a metaphorical way of talking about universal forces in general–is but "the kernel of the perspective view and why a living creature is 'egoistic' through and through." I will have my own say about the will to power in the last chapter, but I say here that the idea that each quantum of force is, or has, or maps onto, a perspective for Nietzsche, seems to me to mean little more than what the passage just quoted says. I had my say in the second chapter as to what I think Nietzsche's perspectivism does come to, but at this level it seems to amount to little more than the triviality that everything, quanta of forces included, has a certain location in space and time that largely determines with what effect it acts on the world.

What, after all, could it mean for a quantum of force to *have* a perspective in any literal sense? Or for there to *be* a perspective that somehow maps onto each quantum of force? To be where or in what? That this idea is not really intelligible does not, of course, mean that Nietzsche didn't hold it (or think himself to hold it). But there is another possibility here in understanding Hales and Welson even if we insist that only conscious beings can have perspectives in the literal sense; namely, that everything is a conscious being. Although they don't make much of it otherwise, they do write that quanta of power "are essentially experience, or, as he [Nietzsche] puts it, a *pathos* . . ." (2000, 63). I present my own understanding of Nietzsche's famous passage in the last chapter, but here I will say only that I believe it is a serious mistake to suppose that Nietzsche believed that everything is conscious or even mental in any sense. And so I reject this possibility of what it could be for everything to have a perspective in Nietzsche.

In introducing their idea of a perspectivist ontology in Nietzsche, Hales and Welshon contrast it to what they call "absolutist" ontologies, which, they assure us, Nietzsche entirely rejected (2000, 58). But just what is an absolutist ontology, and in what sense, if any, does it invite one to ascribe to Nietzsche a "perspectivist" ontology instead? In one sense, an absolutist ontology would be one that countenances "absolute" entities in the sense of ones that are eternal or, somewhat less strongly, ones that are simple (ontological) continuants. In another sense, an absolutist ontology could be one, whatever its content, about which its advocate(s) claims "absolute" certainty. Clearly, Nietzsche rejects absolutist ontologies in both these senses. But Hales and Welshon have something different in mind when they say about his rejection of absolutist ontologies that "Nietzsche's perspectivist strategy is deployed against the distinction between the real and apparent world and the Kantian distinction between the thing-in-itself and appearance" (2000, 58). So we are to understand that, in adopting a "perspectivist" ontology, Nietzsche is rejecting any version of a two-worlds view. And, in this sense too, we may agree that Nietzsche rejects an absolutist ontology. But does this really lead us to ascribe to him what Hales and Welshon mean by a perspectivist ontology?

What could it even possibly mean for something to exist only in the context of a perspective? Although many postmodernists consistently confuse the matter of the certainty (psychological or rational) of a theory with that of the objective reality of its subject matter, it is fairly clear that Hales and Welson are thinking initially, at least, of the subject matter itself when they declare that Nietzsche's perspectivist ontology is more radically anti-realist than any contemporary or any other anti-realism (2000, 75), although the latter also has its sometimes confused epistemological (we can have no knowledge of a mind-independent reality) and ontological (there is no mind-independent reality) aspects. Somehow, for Hales and Welshon, even though the notion of a perspective is primarily an epistemological one, we are to understand it as a component of reality itself but in a way that denies the "absolute", that is, the objective status of that reality. In short, Hales and Welshon appear to have made the confusion of supposing that when someone denies the existence of a reality behind the appearance, one is denying any kind of objective reality, failing to see that the world of appearance itself *is* the reality, and can have, in the strongest sense, an objective and "absolute" reality. Nietzsche himself says as much in, for example, in *The Twilight of the Idols* in summarizing his rejection of a world beyond appearance:

> Any distinction between a "true" and an "apparent" world—whether in the Christian manner or in the manner of Kant (in the end an underhanded Christian)--is only a suggestion of decadence, a symptom of the *decline of life*. That the artist esteems appearance higher than reality is no objection to this proposition. For "appearance" in this case means reality *once more,* only by way of selection, reinforcement, and correction. (TI "'Reason' in Philosophy" 6, Nietzsche's emphases)

"[R]eality *once more*." I conclude that the notion of a "perspectivist" ontology, in any but the trivial sense indicated, is either not intelligible or not Nietzsche's or both.

In much the same context, Hales and Welshon talk about the bundle theory of things in Nietzsche. It is much the same context because, having correctly characterized Nietzsche's notion of the will to power in what I have been calling the cosmic sense as consisting of quanta of a certain sort, they incorrectly claim that "Nietzsche's ontology of objects as structured bundles of power is isomorphic to what contemporary metaphysicians call the bundle theory of objects" (2000, 66) while Welshon, in his article says that "Perspectivist ontology is, pretty obviously, akin to a bundle theory of objects, the thesis that objects are reducible to bundles of properties."

(1999, 41). It is incorrect because it is confusing two kinds of analysis. Analyzing everything into quanta of power is, if it is akin to anything, much more like analyzing everything into the atoms of the physicists. And, I submit, Nietzsche thought of it as an alternative view on the same issue. Analyzing things into bundles of properties is ontological, not scientific or quasi-scientific analysis, as can be seen by considering what I take to be the obvious fact that the scientific analysis of matter is fully consistent with any of the traditional ontologies of things–substance, bare particular, bundle of properties. But while Hales and Welshon somewhat distinguish these two kinds of theories, they nevertheless seem to think that Nietzsche himself was somewhat confused (whereas I think it is their confusion) in saying (2000, 72) that

> With regard to bundle composition he [Nietzsche] wavers between:
> 1. Property composition: the bundles are composed of properties (see *WP* 557, 558); and
> 2. Power composition: the bundles are composed of quanta of power (see *BGE* 36; *WP* 1067).

Still, as we considered earlier in this chapter, Nietzsche was a bundle theorist of things. Furthermore, Hales and Welshon have a detailed discussion of bundle theories and of objections and replies to such theories, being somewhat overly influenced by the assumption that if some version of the theory has serious flaws, then Nietzsche probably didn't hold it. (Much of their discussion has to do with disputing James Van Cleve's objections to the bundle theory. A more incisive criticism of Van Cleve's mostly modal arguments can be found in Albert Casullo's 1987.) And they make the serious, if not entirely uncommon, mistake of supposing that the bare particular theory claims or entails that there are objects without properties (2000, 68), thus incorrectly rejecting this as a possibility for understanding Nietzsche because he, like every other ontologist in the history of philosophy, denies that there are objects without properties. (A particular is bare *not* in having no properties but in having no *essential* properties, that is, in being without a *nature* that, unlike the particulars of the substance tradition, distinguishes it intrinsically and qualitatively from most other particulars. Of course, some ontologists, such as Quine, deny that there are properties altogether, but that is not quite the same thing.)

Hales and Welshon continue in what I regard as their confusion when they raise the important question of what individuates bundles for

Nietzsche by listing (2000, 72) what they regard as three, competing alternatives:

> And with regard to bundle individuation, he [Nietzsche] considers:
> 1. Conjunctivism: every combination of quanta of power is realized as a bundle-thing (see *WP* 568, 635);
> 2. Constellationism: the bundles are individuated by some external perspective (see *WP* 520, 556, 560); and
> 3. Organizationism: the bundles are individuated intrinsically (see *WP* 636).

They then have extensive discussion of each putative alternative, seeming, as one would expect, to conclude that Nietzsche was a conjunctivist. Just before I turned to Hales and Welshon, I considered a possibility of the sort they call organizationism; but now, leaving Hales and Welshon, I want to continue my discussion of Nietzsche's bundle theory by considering something like what they call constellationism, at least with respect to the idea of something external to the object itself.

This is the theory that *we* impose the unity, in thought and language; that *we* organize the otherwise inherently non-bundled properties and relations into the bundles that are ordinary objects. And there are several notes in *The Will to Power*, especially in entries 553-569, that seem to endorse this possibility. Consider, for example, this note (WP 556), dated 1885-1886:

> A "thing-in-itself" just as perverse as a "sense-in-itself," a "meaning-in-itself." There are no "facts-in-themselves," for a sense must always be projected into them before there can be "facts."
> . . .
> The origin of "things" is wholly the work of that which imagines, thinks, wills, feels. (KGW VIII 2 [149, 142])

And in an interesting note of Spring 1887 (WP 560), Nietzsche writes:

> That things possess a constitution in themselves quite apart from interpretation and subjectivity, is a quite idle hypothesis: it presupposes that interpretation and subjectivity are not essential, that a thing freed from all relationships would still be a thing.
> Conversely, the apparent *objective* character of things: could it not be merely a difference of degree within the subjective?–that perhaps that which changes slowly presents itself to us as "objectively" enduring, being, "in-itself"–that the objective is only a false concept of a genus and an antithesis *within* the subjective? (KGW VIII 9 [40], Nietzsche's emphases)

Finally, in another note also dated Spring 1887 (WP 569), we read:

> ... what things "in-themselves" may be like, apart from our sense receptivity and the activity of our understanding, must be rebutted with the question: how could we know that things exist? "Thingness" was first created by us. The question is whether there could not be many other ways of creating such an apparent world–and whether this creating, logicizing, adapting, falsifying is not itself the best-guaranteed reality; in short, whether that which "posits things" is not the sole reality; and whether the "effect of the external world upon us" is not also only the result of such active subjects— The other "entities" act upon us; our adapted apparent world is an adaptation and overpowering of their actions; a kind of defensive measure. The subject alone is demonstrable; hypothesis that only subjects exist–that "object" is only a kind of effect produced by a subject upon a subject–a *modus* of *the subject*. (KGW VIII 9 [106], Nietzsche's emphases)

It would be well to remember, in discussing the ideas of these passages and their relevance to understanding Nietzsche's ontology of physical objects, that these are *notes*, not intended by Nietzsche for publication, even though the material included in *The Will to Power* constitutes his most extensive treatment of the topic in what of his has been published. But it is not my intention in any case to assign to Nietzsche a final, definite ontology in every respect, not just because none is to be found in his writings but also because he was not equipped, so to speak, even to conceive such a detailed ontology insofar as that depends on developments in philosophy, especially in analytic ontology, that were to come only later. But with these *caveats* in mind, we may proceed.

The philosophical theory that we create the objects that are ordinarily taken to be external to the mind is a form of idealism, the broader definition of which is usually that, in some sense or other, everything is mental. The ruminations of *The Will to Power* obviously suggest that Nietzsche was drawn to this form of idealism. And indeed he does sometimes seem to accept also one of the fundamental premises of idealism–that because we cannot be aware of anything of which we are not aware, the existence of anything depends on our awareness of it, that all objects are objects "known" because every object we encounter is "conditioned" by the fact that someone is aware of it. Nietzsche expresses something like this idea in a note dated 1885-1886 (WP 555):

> Coming to know means "to place oneself in a conditional relation to something"; to feel oneself conditioned by something and oneself to condition it–it is therefore under all circumstances establishing, denoting, and making-conscious of conditions (not forthcoming entities, things, what is "in-itself"). (KGW VIII 2 [154])

That what I called a fundamental premise of idealism is false has been so often persuasively argued that I shall not myself also do so except to remark, because it will be relevant in my discussion of Nietzsche's philosophy of mind, and putting aside the trivial fact that we cannot be aware of anything of which we are not aware, that the most important fact to keep in mind is that *the intentional connection is not causally efficacious*, that is, to think of something is not to have an effect on it. It is this piece of commonsense that idealists deny (along with assorted New Agers, transcendental meditationists, some religionists, and others); when I (and now you, as you read these words) think about the planet Mars–billions of years old–we have no effect on it whatsoever. It makes no difference to its properties whether we think of it or not, where *being-thought-of* is not, in the relevant sense, a property of a thing. In short, idealism is false.

Was Nietzsche an idealist then? Do not the passages I quoted and others I could have quoted, although not much from the writings he published or intended for publication, support an affirmative answer? The short answer is that the passages do support an affirmative answer, but Nietzsche was not an idealist. Or, if he was an idealist in fact, it was despite himself. Let me explain myself and, in doing so, strike a more general point, a point that is subtle and difficult to state easily, but one that is, I am convinced, fundamental in understanding Nietzsche.

There is, first of all, the obvious point that any philosopher who, like Nietzsche, makes regular notes to him- or herself, considers possibilities that that philosopher, on further reflection, is not prepared to put into publication or defend further in any other way. Probably this is true to some extent of any philosopher who aspires to add something to the grand dialectic of the Western philosophical tradition. Still, there is a broad coherence of a sort to Nietzsche's ruminations (as I called them), and I do not propose to rest my claim that Nietzsche was not an idealist on this fact about how philosophers often proceed.

My point has to do instead with *contexts*. In the case at hand, it is illustrated by the fact that *whenever the context is just that of the plausibility of idealism, Nietzsche is always on the side of realism and objectivity.* But the general idea can perhaps be better illustrated with another example from Nietzsche. We know that Nietzsche denies that value claims have any ground in external (or any) reality. He expresses this view in *The Twilight of the Idols* in the simple statement that *"there are altogether no moral facts"* (TI "The 'Improvers' of Mankind" 1, Nietzsche's emphasis), adding that "Moral judgments agree with religious ones in believing in realities which are no realities." But if someone were now to say that Nietzsche's claim that there are no moral facts follows from his more general claim that there are no facts at all, that person would have wrongly mixed contexts. For in any context is which Nietzsche says, in these words or others, that there are no moral facts, he is taking for granted, as he should, that *there are non-moral facts*, that is, ordinary empirical facts such as the particular fact that this water is boiling and the general fact that water, when heated to at least 212 degrees Fahrenheit at sea level, boils; and perhaps other kinds of non-moral facts as well.

But what is this matter of contexts? And how does it apply not just to Nietzsche but to philosophical thought in general? I do not wish for a moment to deny–indeed the whole thrust of this essay is the opposite–that a philosopher may be said to have a coherent, comprehensive view of reality that, as it were, goes beyond particular contexts. But I do say that one must always keep in mind, in considering the particular theory that a philosopher is discussing and perhaps advocating what theory or theories he or she is arguing *against*. For what, in one context, will appear to be an endorsement of this or that theory may, in another context appear as a theory to be doubted or rejected. To take yet another example, this time not from Nietzsche: Would it not seem to be an inappropriate mixing of contexts if, when two philosophers, one of whom happened to be a philosophical skeptic, are arguing about which restaurant is farther to walk to, the other philosopher suddenly interjected that because he, the skeptic, holds that we don't know anything anyway, we might as well do it her way. This example may also illustrate that there are philosophical theories that no one really believes, but the skeptic would surely not take the other philosopher's reason as decisive; the context is wrong.

In Nietzsche's case, we have a further complication, and that is his frequent talk, in both the works he intended for publication and the writings he did not, about "perspectives" and "interpretations". I argued earlier, and will not repeat that argument here, that despite all this talk, and sometimes even in light of it, the overall thrust of Nietzsche's thinking is a plea for objectivity, so far best, but never perfectly, exemplified in empirical science, which idea is itself based on the assumption that the world is not, in any significant way, of our making and may well not be in significant accord with our values or our hopes or our tastes or most of our beliefs. Indeed, there are many, many passages in Nietzsche exactly to this point. Further, Nietzsche must and does, to be consistent with his ideal of the *Übermensch* and "overcoming" the prejudices and values and beliefs of ordinary humans, presuppose that we do *not* impose whatever structure reality has, but that it is already there to be *discovered*. This, it is surely as easily understood as said, is fully consistent with the thesis that *how* we categorize and label things is, in part, a matter of our needs and purposes and values and even beliefs; but that is an obvious and trivial "imposition" of the mind on the external reality, whatever Nietzsche sometimes and contemporary "anti-realists" may think.

Many of these distinctions, both of theories and of method, are ones that, very probably, Nietzsche himself rarely, if ever, made clear to himself. And I do believe that he often makes a lot more of the role of the needs and the limits of humans in understanding the world than either the facts he considers or any other facts he might have considered really justify. Nietzsche *does* sometimes skirt dangerously close to idealism, an absurd philosophy. But, as I said above, whenever that is the issue itself, Nietzsche is always unequivocally on the side of realism and objectivity, the latter as both possibility and ideal.

But before we turn to Nietzsche's ontology of mind, we must ask ourselves two questions: Does the bundle theory entail that there are no commonsense continuants, that is, no things? Does the bundle theory entail that, strictly speaking, neither logic nor truth applies to the world?

We saw that the bundle theory has both what we might call a realist version, according to which, in addition to the properties and relations that make up an ordinary object, there is a bundling relation, and an idealist version, according to which minds impose the unity that makes for an ordinary object out of the properties and relations. Nietzsche wavers between these two versions, and I think it would be a mistake to ascribe one or the other to him in any definite way. I would say, however, that even on the idealist version, there is the curious fact that we all, even from previously independent cultures, seem to impose the unity in very much the same way, a fact that ought to give anyone who is tempted by this view very serious pause. For it strongly suggests that there is something in the things themselves (not: the things-in-themselves!) that provides the unity, and the idealist is called upon to say why that suggestion is false.

But I want to insist that whether in the realist version or the idealist version (as long as the imposition is reasonably uniform), there is no good reason for denying that there are commonsense continuants and therefore "things". For either way, there will be a basis for sameness through time, which is what is required for something to be a commonsense continuant. As we know, that basis is sometimes the orbit feature but more often the sameness of properties and relations themselves, not *through* time, but as appearing at different times. And this is the case on any ontology of things, including the substance theory. The substance theorist has a certain *ontology* of strict sameness through time, but that ontology cannot provide our *criteria* of sameness; we do not determine that this is the same ordinary object we saw yesterday by observing that it is, or contains, the same substance. Even if substances were observable as such, we could not do that, for what distinguishes one carrot from another, as far as observation goes, is only its accidents, including possibly the orbit feature. Thus, *whatever the correct ontology of ordinary objects is, our basis for determining sameness through time lies in ordinary criteria of observation.* Thus, too, we are, in any case, entitled to regard ordinary objects as things, which is not, for Nietzsche anyway, as trivial as it sounds. More generally, as with selves, the question is not whether or not ordinary objects exist, but what is their ontological analysis.

Probably the more important question, however, is that concerning logic and truth. And here I think Nietzsche is radically and importantly mistaken. One can, of course, define 'truth' so that it applies only to what is eternal or unchanging, but that is not very interesting. The question is whether or not truth and logic, in their ordinary meanings, apply to ordinary objects, even under the condition of an ontological analysis that involves constant change and denial of substance, perhaps even that of the idealist version of the bundle theory. The answer, I submit, is yes. Let us see.

Truth is a property, in the first instance, of thoughts, and, in the second, of pieces of language. If there were no minds, there would be nothing in the universe with the property of *being-true* or *being-false*. Furthermore, as any dictionary will tell us and therefore putting aside the various so-called theories of truth, a thought that something is the case is true if it is the case: my thought that red is a color is true and is made true by its being the case that red is a color. Put this way, it would seem that that something's being the case could be anything whatsoever, including even the most ephemeral of occurrences. Nietzsche took it to be the case that everything is constantly changing, and if he is right, then the thought that everything is constantly changing is *true*. Furthermore, if it is the case that this leaf is constantly changing, then the thought that this leaf is constantly changing is *true*. And if it is the case that ordinary objects are bundles of their properties and relations, whether held together by a bundling relation or even by the imposition of a mind, then the thought that ordinary objects are bundles of their properties and relations is *true*. And if, therefore, it is the case that this leaf is a bundle of its properties and relations, then the thought that this leaf is a bundle of its properties and relations is *true*. Thus, at this level at least, the theories of constant change and of ordinary objects as bundles are no obstacles to the idea that truth, in its most common and most important sense, has application to reality.

But we may now proceed to observe that if any or all of these circumstances do not obtain, then the corresponding thought is *false*. In short, for example, it is the case either that this leaf is constantly changing or that it is not constantly changing: if the first, then the thought that it is constantly changing is true; if the second, then the same thought is false. Thus, the law of non-contradiction seems to apply perfectly to this situation.

I conclude, tentatively (because there is a further complication to be considered), that it is a mistake to suppose that either the theory of constant change or the theory of ordinary objects as bundles to any extent whatsoever diminishes the full objectivity and mind-independence of the notions of truth and logic and of their application to the world. Thus, Nietzsche (if it is really true of him) and those who would follow him in finding in those theories a basis for (1) denying the existence of an objective reality, or (2) denying that there is an objective truth about the reality, or (3) denying that formal logic applies to that reality are wrong.

But there is a complication. And it is one, whatever Nietzsche made of it, that applies to all ontological theories of ordinary objects even if the substance theorists found themselves somewhat embarrassed by it. And that is the fact that what counts as *an* ordinary object depends in considerable measure on how we *categorize* things. It is very important to see at the outset that this undeniable fact is not the same would-be fact of the idealists, according to which we impose the unity on things. For the first fact, that of categorization, involves no *manipulation* of reality, but only a matter of, so to speak, how we lay words on the world. And this will depend on human perception, human needs, human desires, human values, and probably other things human as well. For the most part, when we think of paradigmatic examples of ordinary objects, we think of objects that "drag" most of their parts around with them. So a carrot is a thing, a star is a thing, and a person is a thing. But then, their parts are also things, and for mostly the same reason. Thus, in the case of a person, an arm is a thing, a heart is a thing, and so on.

But, beyond the paradigms, we might say that everything is a thing. My desk and the computer on it are a thing, the book on the desk and the planet Mars are a thing, the universe is a thing, and so on and on. These facts, mostly anthropological, do perhaps cast some doubt on the substance ontology of things; and some substance philosophers have worried their problem of how to guarantee the "definiteness" of substance, so to speak, and what is presumably their definite and finite number at a time. There is also the fact that how we group whatever things we have names for is a matter of anthropology, not ontology. If it were the case, for example, that the near presence of red things were a danger for human beings, we would certainly have a substantive–maybe 'redders' in English–for such objects.

All of these facts, and others like them, indicate what is meant by saying that how we categorize the world we perceive is our doing. The fact, if it is a fact, that there are an infinite number of ways to categorize the world we perceive (even if, in anthropological fact, all cultures categorize in almost but not quite exactly the same ways) is entirely consistent with the fact that the world we perceive is wholly mind-independent, even if, further, how we categorize itself affects how we perceive it. We know the latter to be true, to some extent, but we know it because we are able to see through and beyond it, so to speak, which itself presupposes the fact of a mind-independent reality.

This is, of course, only the lightest sketch of an argument that, even if Nietzsche's ontology of physical objects is correct, the notions of truth and logic, in their strictest objective senses, still apply to the world. For even if, in some sense, it is arbitrary that we pick out this piece of reality and call it a carrot, it is still an objective, mind-independent fact that this carrot is one meter from this tomato, even if, too, the facts that we pick out this distance to call a meter and this piece of reality to call a tomato are also arbitrary
.

Nietzsche had a legitimate and largely correct complaint to make against both the two-worlds view of reality and the substance ontology of ordinary objects. But he carried his opposition too far in rejecting the possibility– the fact, I say–that in rejecting both a world of permanence altogether and of semi-permanent objects in this world that the ordinary notions of truth, logic, and objectivity still apply. On the contrary, like anyone who would argue against the applicability of these notions to the world we live in, he entirely presupposes them. And, as we know, in contexts in which he is arguing against idealists and defending empirical science as the best approach to knowledge of reality, Nietzsche endorses them.

Let us turn to Nietzsche's philosophy of mind.

MINDS

Nietzsche's philosophy of mind, in a broad sense, encompasses many topics that today are rarely considered at all by philosophers, much less in that highly specialized area that is known as philosophy of mind. Even though, in a somewhat technical sense, Nietzsche denies the efficacy of mind, there is much in his writing on the origin, nature, and role of consciousness in human affairs, especially as it is sometimes treating as comprising, sometimes as in opposition to, instinct. These aspects of Nietzsche's philosophy of mind, perhaps better called philosophical anthropology, I shall largely ignore, partly because they are not really, in the sense I have adumbrated, a part of his ontology, partly because they have been extensively and very adequately dealt with elsewhere, especially by Richard Schacht (1983, 268-279).

Similarly, I shall largely ignore those themes in Nietzsche that can be alluded to in brief as those of the relations of reason and passion, the nature of the *Übermensch*, pain and pleasure and their roles in human consciousness and behavior, and the nature and role of values in the human mind. All of these matters are widely discussed in the literature, and while what I do have to say may be relevant to our understanding of Nietzsche on them, I shall not myself discuss them directly. My focus, instead, is on more technical aspects of philosophy of mind as they do, or may, pertain to Nietzsche, aspects of his thought that are little or not at all discussed in the literature, to my knowledge.

What is a mind? On my view, which I have developed in many writings (see especially 1989, 5-8), the mind is best understood as comprised of entities from three categories: conscious mental states, dispositional mental states, and things that are *dependent* on conscious mental states for their existence but not *constituents* of such states, such as bodily sensations, emotions, moods, images and afterimages, and perhaps more. But the "essence" of mind is, surely, consciousness—that stream of awareness each of us has at almost all times. And while Nietzsche, like all of us, often uses the word 'consciousness' to include dispositional mental states as well, we may—as I hope will become obvious—largely restrict ourselves to conscious mental states, although we must also somehow include in our discussion, as we must in the ontology of mind itself, the notion of the unconscious. That notion, however, I propose to examine only very late in my discussion of Nietzsche's ontology of mind, for reasons that my own ideas will make clear (I hope).

But we should begin with the observation that, as a very general but crucially important feature of Nietzsche's philosophy of mind, he tends to depreciate the value and importance of consciousness in human affairs. This is again, in part, his placing consciousness in opposition to instinct and his various musings to the effect that civilization has depreciated the importance of instinct. It is also connected with his complex views about values according to which, on the one hand, value permeates all of our thinking while, on the other, a too-respectful view of consciousness is somehow connected with the false belief in absolute values. But it also has a more precise and technical aspect, as I shall argue below.

We should also take note, in these still preliminary remarks, of Nietzsche's general emphasis on the primacy of the body, both epistemologically and ontologically. Some of his notes at least hint at these notions, especially these dated 1885-87 (WP 489, 491, 492, respectively):

> The phenomenon of the body is the richer, clearer, more tangible phenomenon: to be discussed first, methodologically, without coming to any decision about its ultimate significance. (KGW VIII 5 [56])

> Belief in the body is more fundamental than belief in the soul: the latter arose from unscientific reflection on [the agonies of] the body (something that leaves it. Belief in the truth of dreams--). (KGW VIII 2 [102])

> The body and physiology the starting point: why?-- We gain the correct idea of the nature of our subject-unity, namely as regents at the head of a communality . . . (KGW VII 40 [21])

Here, as so often elsewhere, and correctly (I say), Nietzsche takes entirely for granted the existence of bodies and the external world as existing independent of minds. Like everyone, in practice anyway, he is a commonsense realist. At the same time, we should keep in mind his claim that it is the belief in mind as a substance that somehow leads to the belief in physical objects as substances. In that sense, he seems to accord the mind a kind of epistemological priority, however—in his view—mistaken it is in its operation.

As a final general observation, let us take note of Nietzsche's frequently-expressed doubt, at least in the notes of *The Will to Power*, that we really can gain knowledge of the mind. This is *not* because of some cosmic skepticism on his part or because of some kind of relativism or perspectivism, but because of features peculiar to mind or at least to our means of observing it. For example, in a note of 1886-87 (WP 472) he writes:

> Contradiction of the alleged "facts of consciousness." Observation is a thousand times more difficult, error perhaps a condition of observation in general. (KGW VIII 9 [1])

And in a note of 1888 (WP 523), he laments:

> When we observe only the inner phenomena we may be compared with the deaf-and-dumb, who divine through movements of the lips the words they do not hear. From the phenomena of the inner sense we conclude the existence of invisible and other phenomena that we would apprehend if our means of observation were adequate and that one calls the nerve current.
> We lack any sensitive organs for this inner world, so we sense a thousandfold complexity as a unity . . . (KGW VIII 14 [144,145])

This skepticism about what is usually called introspection as a reliable source of knowledge about the nature of consciousness and the mind I shall also give a somewhat more precise formulation as we proceed. And while this expressed skepticism should perhaps give pause to anyone who would presume to find in, or to ascribe to, Nietzsche any definite philosophy of mind, I am now ready to do just that.

The main features of Nietzsche's ontology of mind are these: (1) the mind is not a substance; but (2) the mind is a something that is not, or at least not wholly, physical; and (3) the mind is not causally efficacious, although there is the appearance of such causality. To put labels on these three features, we may say that, with respect to mind, Nietzsche was an anti-substantialist, a dualist, and a parallelist of the ephiphenomenalist variety. The last of these, his epiphenomenalism, is not, strictly speaking, a matter of ontology insofar as it concerns not so much what is, but what causes or fails to cause what. But it derives from his views on what is often considered an ontological matter—the question of which of mind and matter is primary to the other, if either—as well as his views on the nature of causation itself, an issue that is not a matter of fundamental ontology but nonetheless of great metaphysical importance. And, let us again keep in mind for later discussion that there is the matter of the unconscious to be dealt with.

That Nietzsche is an anti-substantialist with respect to mind, as he is with respect to everything, is hardly news, and completely uncontroversial, as far as I know. That he is a dualist of some sort—perhaps what we would now call a property-dualist—is less obvious but probably would be more or less acceptable to most readers and interpreters of Nietzsche. But I may be the first to suggest that he is also a parallelist of the epiphenomenalist variety, and that such a supposition is the best understanding of certain crucial passages, especially in his last work of ontological important intended for publication, *The Twilight of the Idols*. But let us take up these matters in order, following some further texts and discussion of Nietzsche's rejection of any infallibility thesis with regard to mind.

We took note earlier of some notes that appear in *The Will to Power*; but in his works intended for publication, Nietzsche gives more refined expression to his rejection of what we now often call the "transparency-of-mind" thesis: that by introspection each of us has direct and infallible awareness of our own mind that is, or results in, indefeasible beliefs about it. Let us begin with a look at this lengthy passage from *Beyond Good and Evil*:

> There are still harmless self-observers who believe that there are "immediate certainties"; for example, "I think," or as the superstition of Schopenhauer put it, "I will"; as though knowledge here got hold of its object purely and nakedly as "the thing in itself," without any falsification on the part of either the subject or the object. But that "immediate certainty," as well as "absolute knowledge" and the "thing in itself," involve a *contradictio in adjecto*, I shall repeat a hundred times; we really ought to free ourselves from the seduction of words!
> Let the people suppose that knowledge means knowing things entirely; the philosopher must say to himself: When I analyze the process that is expressed by the sentence, "I think," I find a whole series of daring assertions that would be difficult, perhaps impossible, to prove; for example, that it is *I* who think, that there must necessarily be something that thinks, that thinking is an activity and operation on the part of a being who is thought of as a cause, that there is an "ego," and, finally, that it is already determined what is to be designated by thinking—that I *know* what thinking is. For if I had not already decided within myself what it is, by what standard could I determine whether that which is just happening is not perhaps "willing" or "feeling"? In short, the assertion "I

think" assumes that I *compare* my state at the present moment with other states of myself which I know, in order to determine what it is; on account of this retrospective connection with further "knowledge," it has, at any rate, no immediate certainty for me. (BGE 16, Nietzsche's emphases)

We see in this passage Nietzsche's rejection of the mind as a substance, to which matter I shall turn shortly. But the primary point is to reject certain *categories* of putative entities as certain ones that comprise the mind, even though, in many other contexts, he invokes them himself without hesitation. Part of his worry could be expressed, somewhat as Wilfrid Sellars was to do nearly a century later, by saying that the way we understand something is as a member of a certain category of things. So the idea that we are directly given something as a certain thing—that is, as a certain *kind* of thing—is at least dubious. Another way of saying very much the same thing is to observe that to identify something as a certain thing is, as Nietzsche says in the passage, at least implicitly to *compare* it with objects of one's earlier experiences, and so again is not merely the result of one's present awareness of it. Some have expressed this aspect of a rejection of the transparency-of-mind thesis by saying that direct awareness is not, by itself, knowledge at all, but only just that—awareness. Knowledge involves categories and comparisons and, one might add, durations that are more than momentary awarenesses.

But of course there is also quite another, though related, aspect to the issue of the transparency of mind. And that is the question of whether or not one could be completely mistaken about what seems to be the nature and object of one's awareness. (Of course, one can be mistaken in what one thinks or believes about the object of one's awareness.) Could I be mistaken, for example, in thinking that I now have a headache—when I am instead having great pleasure? Or that I am now thinking of my daughters when, *instead* (not in addition to), I am really perceiving the far side of the moon? Some contemporary philosophers have suggested that even matters like these are not certain; and, indeed, given their ontologies of mind, probably are committed to some such views. I take such consequences to be a *reduction ad absurdum* of those ontologies. It is, perhaps, not so much a matter of having some kind of absolute guarantee that one is really having the state of awareness one takes oneself to be having so much as the fact that any kind of communication, including that with oneself, presupposes that to be so. And that applies to philosophical discourse as well: when a philosopher says that we cannot be certain that we are having the states of awareness we take ourselves to be having, he is wholly presupposing that he himself *is* having the state of awareness he takes himself to be having. This fact is just a specific form of the argument against skepticism in general that any argument in favor of skepticism presupposes its falsity by necessarily invoking some premises that must be known to be true if the conclusion is to be accepted as true or even plausible.

But where does Nietzsche stand in all of this? As is so often the case, despite his provocative remarks in both his writings intended for publication and those not—some of which I have quoted—we are not in a position to ascribe any of the kind of very specific views that later philosophers have developed. I have noted his apparent anticipation of some views later stated and developed by Ludwig Wittgenstein, Wilfrid Sellars, Richard Rorty, and others; but that does not get us very far. So, having taken note in this lengthy way of Nietzsche's skepticism about knowledge of the mind that does *not* derive from his alleged skepticism about any kind of knowledge, I proceed finally to the three major features of his ontology of mind.

The mind is not a substance. There is no substantial self. There is no simple entity that persists through the existence of a person's mind in time. In the present context, these are all ways of saying the same thing; and Nietzsche's rejection of the substance view of mind hardly sets him apart many philosophers both before and after his time. But it is important in this connection to note that most contemporary philosophers who hold that, as the crucial constituent of a mind, there is a simple entity that persists through time, do not necessarily, and need not, also hold to most of the other traditional features of substance that I identified in the last chapter. They may well treat this entity as the ultimate subject of properties in the case of being a mind, but they are likely to reject, or at least to ignore, most or all of the other features.

As for predecessors to Nietzsche, David Hume is almost certainly the most famous and most important in denying the substantialist theory of mind and, very possibly, his view comes closest to Nietzsche's among those predecessors. But in quite a different way, there is also the case of Benedict Spinoza who, in saying that all "finite modes" (that is, all ordinary temporal objects including minds) are not substances was emphasizing, above all, their lack of ontological independence, all of them being, ultimately, modes of the one and only substance which he called God or the whole of nature itself. Having next to nothing to say about the ontological analysis of ordinary objects (a serious defect, in my opinion, of this otherwise great philosopher's innovative thinking), Spinoza cannot really be held to be either affirming or denying that such an object, whether physical or mental, has a persistent entity as a constituent. Nietzsche was an admirer of Spinoza, but in the respects he mentions in which he sees him as anticipating his own views, he does not mention the nature of the mind except in the denial of the freedom of the will. (Not incidentally to our general purposes, however, Nietzsche says, in a letter to his friend, Franz Overbeck, that Spinoza's "over-all tendency" is like his in "making knowledge the *most powerful* affect" (Kaufmann, 1954, 92, Nietzsche's emphasis), whatever exactly that means.)

But in a note of 1887 (WP 484), Nietzsche reasonably cites Descartes as one who tried to supply a philosophical basis for the idea of the self as substance:

> "There is thinking: therefore there is something that thinks": this is the upshot of all Descartes' argumentation. But that means positing as "true *a priori*" our belief in the concept of substance—that when there is thought there has to be something "that thinks" is simply a formulation of our grammatical custom that adds a doer to every deed. In short, this is not merely the substantiation of a fact but a logical-metaphysical postulate--Along the lines followed by Descartes one does not come upon something absolutely certain but only upon the fact of a very strong belief. (KGW VIII 10 [158])

More precisely, as Nietzsche puts it in another note, also of 1887 (WP 488):

> The logical-metaphysical postulates, the belief in substance, accident, attribute, etc., derive their convincing force from our habit of regarding all our deeds as consequences of our will—so that the ego, as substance, does not vanish in the multiplicity of change.—But there is no such thing as will.-- (KGW VIII 9 [98])

To this final claim I shall turn separately later. For now, I observe that there are many other notes in *The Will to Power* to the same effect as those I've quoted, especially in entries 481-492. But we should also look at a passage from *Twilight of the Idols* in which much the same idea is expressed, a passage that also involves some ideas from the last chapter:

> Formerly, alteration, change, any becoming at all, were taken as proof of mere appearance, as an indication that there must be something which led us astray. Today, conversely, precisely insofar as the prejudice of reason forces us to posit unity, identity, permanence, substance, cause, thinghood, being, we see ourselves somehow caught in error, compelled into error. So certain are we, on the basis of rigorous examination, that this is where the error lies.
>
> It is no different in this case than with the movement of the sun: there our eye is the constant advocate of error, here it is our language. In its origin language belongs in the age of the most rudimentary form of psychology. We enter a realm of crude fetishism when we summon before consciousness the basic presuppositions of the metaphysics of language, in plain talk, the presuppositions of reason. Everywhere it sees a doer and doing; it believes in will as *the* cause; it believes in the ego, in the ego as being, in the ego as substance, and it projects this faith in the ego-substance upon all things—only thereby does it first *create* the concept of "thing." Everywhere "being" is projected by thought, pushed underneath, as the cause; the concept of being follows, and is a derivative of, the concept of ego. (TI "'Reason' in Philosophy" 5, Nietzsche's emphases)

Again, against those (perhaps including Nietzsche himself!) who say that Nietzsche's view is that we have no knowledge at all or that everything is relative in some interesting sense or the like, we see that, in the perfectly everyday sense, he takes certain facts for granted, being now established by empirical science; for example, that the sun does not move around the earth. And of course in speaking of the errors of unity, identity, and so on, he presupposes the truth of their denials, which is his own view. But that is not our present theme, important though it be to give it frequent restatement.

We may also take note, for later purposes, of Nietzsche's (surely false) view that language falsely "believes" in the will as the *only* cause, very strongly implying *not* what he seems to hold in other contexts—that there are no causes or that the notion of cause is projected by us on the world or that the will to power (which is *not* the ordinary human will) is the only cause—but that there are other causes in addition to, or instead of, the will. To this matter, I shall also turn shortly. But of course it is tied to his rejection of the self or the mind as a substance insofar as he seems to connect our belief in such a theory with the belief that we, or even we alone, are the causes of what happens. While it is true that some philosophers, most notably George Berkeley, held that only a mental substance can be a cause of anything whatsoever, I think we must say that here Nietzsche's historical and psychological diagnosis of the belief in mind as substance is dubious in the extreme. I would rather say that the substance ontology, in its application to both physical objects and to minds, is the natural first theory that philosophy would be expected to come up with, being rooted in our everyday experience of the world; and that language, far from being the cause of the belief in this ontology, is instead one of its effects. This is not to say that the substance ontology is true; and in the last chapter I indicated what I take to be adequate reasons for thinking it to be false.

But the important point for us here is Nietzsche's rejection of the substantialist theory of the mind. And his primary reason, somewhat but not entirely obscured by his method, is the best reason; namely, that we are not acquainted with any such entity in our experience—in this case, by introspection. And while invoking this fact may not be entirely consistent with his rejection of the transparency theory of mind, it is nevertheless the fundamental reason any anti-substantialist should have, combined with the further claim that the "unity" of the mind that we do experience, the sense of self that the normal human mind does have, can be fully accommodated on an ontology that recognizes no simple, persistent entities. As I like to put it: the question is not whether or not there is such a thing as the self but, instead, what is its ontological analysis.

So much then for the first of the three main features of Nietzsche's ontology of mind. Let us move on to the second, his dualism of mind and body.

The tradition generally recognizes three broad positions regarding mind and matter, that is, of those entities that, presumably, exhaust the particular things in space and time: the idealist holds that everything is mental and that the physical is as aspect of the mental; the materialist holds that everything is physical and that the mental is an aspect of the physical; the dualist holds that some things are mental and some things are physical and that at least one of each sort is not an aspect of the other sort. I have used this vague word 'aspect' to cover many different ways in which the relation of the mental and the physical has been conceived. Furthermore, there is an asymmetry in how various views are categorized insofar as that according to which the physical is *causally* dependent on the mental is regarded as a form of idealism even if there remains a genuine distinction between what is primarily mental and the physical; whereas the widely-held view (also Nietzsche's, I believe) according to which the mental is *causally* dependent on the physical while there remains a genuine distinction between what is primarily physical and the mental is usually regarded as a form of dualism. (Cutting things finer, we may distinguish several forms—or meanings, if you prefer—of materialism, in which this form of dualism is also called scientific materialism in contrast to absolute or philosophical or ontological materialism.) And one must also keep in mind that almost every ontologist of mind, even the most committed dualist, would agree that some things we regard as mental—dispositional mental states, for example—are, ontologically speaking, physical.

What, then, are Nietzsche's views on these matters? Is he really an idealist, as we know some notes that appear in *The Will to Power* (and elsewhere) suggest? Or is he really a materialist, insofar as in some passages we have seen and others we will see, he seems to deny the efficacy and even the existence of mind or at least of the will, sometimes in favor of the physiological, and for other reasons as well? As for a clear and direct statement on Nietzsche's part on this issue, one will look in vain, at least in my experience. We do know that many of his harshest statements about other philosophers are directed at idealists of some sort or other, including Leibniz, Berkeley, Kant, Hegel, and Schopenhauer. (Of course, he also had much good to say about Leibniz and Schopenhauer.) It is a further fact that many of his actual uses of the word 'idealism' ('idealismus' in German) have to do with that other major sense concerning values or outlook. And it would seem to be a mistake of the first order to suppose, as many commentators seem to have supposed, that rejection of the thing-in-itself as an unknowable or at least unobservable something or other entails rejection of a mind-independent reality, observable and knowable in part. Opposition to another world or to a hidden part of this world that would, if it existed, be independent of minds does not require opposition to anything whatsoever that is independent of mind such as the everyday objects of perception, which is exactly what commonsense realism holds.

I have already granted that there are many passages in Nietzsche, especially in his notes, that might lead one to take him as an idealist. But whenever he himself uses the word, it is to reject whatever it is that he there understands by it. We can be quite confident that he himself would reject the label as applicable to him, but that is, to be sure, by no means conclusive. The situation may be similar to that of those twentieth-century phenomenalists (with whom I have already compared Nietzsche) who maintained that all physical-object statements could be analyzed (that is, restated without loss of cognitive meaning) with reference only to actual sense data, thought of as dependent on the mind of a perceiver, and would-be sense data (that is, sense data the perceiver would have of the "same" object in different circumstances). Insofar as this ontology appears to be one in which the only existents are mind (however themselves treated) and sense data, it would seem to be one in which, in a strong sense, everything is mental. So were these philosophers, some of them members of the Vienna Circle, idealists? They would vehemently have denied it. Perhaps we should look at the matter from a different "perspective."

One fact that should very much lead us away from thinking of Nietzsche as an idealist is his fondness for physiological explanations. In fact, in general—a matter I will take up in a more specific form later—Nietzsche is disposed, when it comes to everyday, scientific explanations of both thought and behavior, to appeal to the body, that is, to physiological factors. For example, in *Beyond Good and Evil* he writes of grounding our values in physiology as follows:

> Behind all logic and its seeming sovereignty of movement, too, there stand valuations or, more clearly, physiological demands for the preservation of a certain type of life. For example, that the definite should be worth more than the indefinite, and mere appearance worth less than "truth"—such estimates might be, in spite of their regulative importance for *us*, mere foreground estimates, a certain kind of *niaiserie* which may be necessary for the preservation of just such beings as we are. (BGE 3, Nietzsche's emphases)

In a note of 1886-87 (WP 408), Nietzsche includes physiology as something the knowledge of which philosophers lack, presumably indicating its importance to understanding the world:

> What do philosophers lack? (a) an historical sense, (b) knowledge of physiology, (c) a goal in the future-- The ability to formulate a critique without any irony or moral condemnation. (KGW VII 26 [100])

And in another note, this one from 1887 (WP 117), which is worth quoting in full for its richness and relevance to our broader theme, Nietzsche also indicates the primacy of the body:

> Progress of the nineteenth century against the eighteenth (--at bottom *we good Europeans* wage a war against the eighteenth century--):
> 1. "Return to nature" understood more and more decisively in the opposite sense from Rousseau's. *Away from idyl and opera!*
> 2. more and more decisively anti-idealistic, more concrete, more fearless, industrious, moderate, suspicious against sudden changes, *antirevolutionary*;
> 3. more and more decisively the question concerning the *health of the body* is put ahead of that of "the soul": the latter being understood as a state consequent upon on the former, and the former at the very least as a precondition of the health of the soul. (KGW VIII 9 [121], Nietzsche's emphases)

Yet more generally, we know of Nietzsche's determination to see human beings as products of nature, as part of the natural order of things, even if he had doubts about Darwin's particular account of how we came to be as a species (that is, of natural selection as the primary mechanism of evolutionary change). Nor can we doubt that Nietzsche believed that the physical universe existed long before there was any consciousness of any degree. (Some idealists claim to be able to accommodate this obvious truth in some way or other.) Despite all of his attacks on the traditional notions of science, truth, knowledge, and reality, Nietzsche was prepared largely to accept the commonsense realist view of the world, as elaborated by empirical science. This attitude is most evident in *Twilight of the Idols*, but it is there in all of his mature writings intended for publication as well as in the notes collected as *The Will to Power*.

Is Nietzsche then a materialist? It is true that he has Zarathustra say that "soul is only a word for something about the body" (Z I "On the Despisers of the Body"), but one might well connect such words with Aristotle's claim that the mind is the "form" of the body, a claim that in historical fact led eventually to the substance-dualism of Descartes. Still, this passage and others I have quoted above and yet others I could have quoted very much support taking Nietzsche as holding to *the primacy of the body* with respect to mind, being both a causal and an ontological primacy. Yet, despite what some contemporary philosophers imagine, such a view is not yet materialism in the sense of mind's being only some part or feature or aspect or undertaking of the body. In the only passage I have found in which Nietzsche uses the word 'materialism' ('materialismus' in German), he might well be read as making exactly the distinction I am making between the mind's being *dependent* on the body and the mind's being *the same thing* as the body (or, more precisely, a part or aspect thereof). This passage appears in *The Genealogy of Morals*:

> A strong and well-constituted man digests his experiences (his deeds and misdeeds included) as he digests his meals, even when he has to swallow some tough morsels. If he cannot get over an experience and have done with it, this kind of indigestion is as much physiological as is the other—and often in fact merely a consequence of the other.—With such a conception one can, between ourselves, still be the sternest opponent of all materialism.--) (GM Third Essay 16)

I think we may safely say that, despite his words, Nietzsche is at least a scientific materialist; that is, that everything that happens, including all mental life, has a physical explanation. For some philosophers, this is taken, if not to entail, at least to make likely (if it is true), what is variously called absolute or philosophical or ontological materialism, that is, that everything that exists is physical. I am with Nietzsche in believing these philosophers to be mistaken—that one can hold to the primacy of the physical realm, indeed its exclusivity with respect to causal explanation, without denying the existence of a distinct realm of mental entities. We know that this realm is devoid of substances for Nietzsche, but beyond that he gives us little to go on. I have already suggested, for whatever help it may give us, that we may imagine his conception of mind to be similar to Hume's. What we can say, more definitively, is that Nietzsche, if he is a dualist at all, is a property-dualist only and not a Cartesian-dualist.

But some of this will become clearer if we move on to what I called the third major feature of Nietzsche's ontology of mind, his parallelism. And for this and related matters, I begin with a longish quote from *Twilight of the Idols*:

> We believed ourselves to be causal in the act of willing: we thought that here at least we caught causality in the act. Nor did one doubt that all the antecedents of an act, its causes, were to be sought in consciousness and would be found there once sought—as "motives": else one would not have been free and responsible for it. Finally, who would have denied that a thought is caused? that the ego causes the thought?
> Of these three "inward facts" which seem to guarantee causality, the first and most persuasive is that of the will as cause. The conception of a consciousness ("spirit") as a cause, and later also that of the ego as cause (the "subject"), are only afterbirths: first the causality of the will was firmly accepted as given, as *empirical*.
> Meanwhile we have thought better of it. Today we no longer believe a word of all this. The "inner world" is full of phantoms and will-o'-the-wisps: the will is

one of them. The will no longer moves anything, hence does not explain anything either—it merely accompanies events; it can also be absent. The so-called *motive*: another error. Merely a surface phenomenon of consciousness, something alongside the deed that is more likely to cover up the antecedents of the deeds than to represent them. And as for the *ego*! That has become a fable, a fiction, a play on words: it has altogether ceased to think, feel, or will!

What follows from this? There are no mental causes at all. The whole of the allegedly empirical evidence for that has gone to the devil. That is what follows! (TI "The Four Great Errors" 3, Nietzsche's emphases)

Nietzsche's three "inward facts" perhaps should be restated, if somewhat awkwardly, as (1) the will is the cause of behavior, (2) motives are the causes of what one wills, and (3) the ego is the cause of one's motives. He claims that the first is the crucial one, the other two derivative. We must be careful not to suppose that the general point of this passage is to deny causation altogether, as Nietzsche sometimes does seem to do elsewhere. No, it is exactly what he says in the final paragraph—that there are no *mental* causes. And it is important also to stress that he is not denying the existence of mental phenomena, as is evident from his claim that the will does not cause but only accompanies events and that it can be absent as well (presumably from what are nevertheless to be regarded as voluntary behaviors). So what is going on here?

A philosopher who affirms the existence but denies the efficacy of mental events is an epiphenomenalist, and it seems clear that Nietzsche qualifies for this label. In fact, one can take the claim that there are no mental causes, even though mental phenomena exist, as a rejection of both idealism and materialism, for it directly contradicts idealism while, in denying efficacy to mental phenomena, also denies their identity with physical phenomena. Whether or not Nietzsche saw all of this, I nevertheless offer it as evidence of his dualism.

But there is much more to say about this matter, especially with respect to Nietzsche's claim of accompaniment. For it is this fact that gives the appearance of causality more than anything else. And this, I submit, entitles us, as I suggest some pages back, to regard Nietzsche as a parallelist as well as an epiphenomenalist. For, in principle, one could hold that mental phenomenal exist but have no systematic connection of any kind with any physical phenomena. I doubt that anyone has ever seriously held, much less defended, such a view. Perhaps the beliefs that come closest to it are those of certain kinds of religious fatalists, but even with them it is more the inefficacy of behavior than thought that seems to be emphasized. We know, too, that Nietzsche likes to regard himself as a certain kind of fatalist, but this in no way derives, as far as I can see, from his much more specific thesis about the inefficacy of mental phenomena. It is, instead, more a rejection of teleological worldviews combined with a general understanding that the course of nature, writ large, is not a matter of human, or any other, choice. So let us look at what is involved in parallelism, the modern view, I suggest, that comes closest to what Nietzsche, perhaps somewhat vaguely, had in mind (so to speak).

Parallelism is the thesis that for every mental state there is a temporally simultaneous and lawfully corresponding physical state. In us, that corresponding physical state is a state of the brain, as a matter of empirical fact. And by a mental state, we mean here, most emphatically, a component of the stream of consciousness, such as perceiving a book, a feeling of the pressure of the chair, a headache, a thought of what is going to happen later in the day, an intention to get a drink of water, and the like. The most important immediate implication of parallelism is that for any behavior of a person there will be, to whatever extent that behavior has a lawful explanation, a fully physical explanation of it. Negatively put, if parallelism is true, one *need* not invoke the mind in the explanation of any behavior, if one knew all the relevant initial conditions and all the relevant laws. Many people, including some philosophers, find this idea disturbing. Yet, it follows also from another way of stating the general ideal of parallelism that seems almost commonsensical; namely, that two persons with identical bodily states including brain states at a moment would have, as a matter of lawful necessity, identical mental states at that moment. For put this way, the idea seems to be what is generally assumed in many kinds of practices, especially those of medicine, such as, for example, the use of anesthetics. General anesthesia is the limiting case, in which, by putting the brain in a certain state by the use of certain chemicals, consciousness ceases for the time being. But of course deliberately altering consciousness with the use of chemicals including, most prominently, alcoholic beverages, is as ancient as it is familiar. And the success of such practices rests on the fact of, if not a strict lawful correspondence of mental to bodily states, something very close to it.

In any case, I submit that supposing Nietzsche to have held some such view is the best way to account for the contents not only of the passage just cited but also of numerous others in which he is eager to deny the efficacy of the mind or, more narrowly, of the will or of consciousness. For, on the one hand, and to repeat, an idealist obviously must affirm most emphatically the efficacy of the mind in whatever changes take place in whatever world there is for that theory; indeed, as in Berkeley, he may insist that only the mind is ontologically possible as a cause. And, on the other hand, a materialist, in holding that the mental is the same thing as something physical, can and probably will allow the efficacy of the mental just insofar as it just is a feature of the brain itself or a disposition to behavior. So, in denying efficacy to the mental while not denying its existence (as some extreme materialists—the so-called eliminative ones—do), one seems to be an epiphenomalist. And in affirming the appearance but not the fact of causality, as Nietzsche does, one seems to be a parallelist.

And we can further substantiate Nietzsche's adherence to some such view by taking note of the fact that parallelism, when combined with an assumption that Nietzsche holds, entails that the physical world is, as one says, "causally closed." That assumption is that the physical and mental realms are jointly exhaustive of the spatial-temporal world (indeed, of reality). That means that everything that happens in the physical world has whatever degree of explanation it does have (a "full" explanation in a deterministic world, which is Nietzsche's) by way of other occurrences in the physical world. This is the more general thesis of the one just discussed with respect to the explanation of human behavior. And Nietzsche does seem also to subscribe to the more general thesis.

But parallelism, even while denying the necessity (emphatically, I do not say the *possibility*) of mention of the mind in the explanation of behavior, at the same time accounts for the fact that *it seems as if* our mental states are, at least in part, productive of our behaviors: it certainly seems as if, when I go to the fountain and have a drink of water, that it is *because* I felt thirst, *because* I wanted to eliminate that thirst, and *because* I decided to act in a way toward that end. And feeling thirsty, wanting not to be thirsty, and willing to walk to the fountain and drink water are all mental states. And because, on the thesis of parallelism, all of these mental states do occur at the time they would occur if they were genuinely productive of the behaviors involved, the fact of their seeming to be genuinely productive is at least not puzzling.

Or is it? It is important to understand, however, that some parallelists (myself included) believe that *it seems as if* our mental states are partly involved in the production of our behaviors because our mental states *are* involved in the production of our behaviors. While some critics of parallelism insist that it entails epiphenomenalism—the denial of efficacy to mental states—the fact is that, far from entailing the denial of efficacy, parallelism, *combined with a certain theory of causation*, entails that our mental states are partly productive of our behavior without, however, denying that the physical world is causally closed and that, therefore, interactionism is false. (Interactionism is the thesis that mental states are *necessary* for the explanation of some events in the physical world, that is, that the physical world is not causally closed.) For, on the parallelist's thesis, the laws connecting mental states, brain states, and behaviors are such that, if certain mental states did not occur, then certain brain states and certain behaviors would not occur: if I did not have the mental state of feeling thirsty, then my brain would not be in the state (or one of the states) it needs to be in so that, by the relevant laws, my behavior of walking to the fountain and drinking water will occur. (For greater detail on this point, see Addis, 1984.) Someone may object that even so, on this hypothesis, if the mental states were not there at all, everything would be the same in the physical world, including human bodies, brain states, and behaviors. The proper reply to this objection is that in our world, given the laws that in fact obtain, that is not the case while, in a world with different laws from ours, that might be the case. But so what?

So, what is the theory of causation that, combined with parallelism, entails the efficacy and not the denial of the efficacy of mental states with respect to behavior? It is, as will be obvious to many, that causation is lawful connection and nothing more (or, as I like to say, lawful connection plus "context"; but context is nothing, ontologically speaking). The laws of our universe make it impossible for certain behaviors to occur in human beings unless certain mental states occur or, a little less strongly put, the behaviors that do in fact occur would not have occurred unless certain mental states had occurred. Typically, a philosopher takes for granted the commonsense thesis that what goes on our mind makes a difference to our behaviors, that is, causes them, in least in part. So, if a philosopher believes, for whatever reasons and with whatever theory of causation implicitly or explicitly held, that parallelism entails epiphenomenalism, that philosopher will almost certainly reject parallelism. Nietzsche, as we know, is not, in the relevant sense, a typical philosopher. So he is willing to reject the commonsense thesis, as he does explicitly in the passage I quoted above from *The Twilight of the Idols*, and upon which I have rested much of my discussion. I rested my attribution of parallelism on his talk of the "accompaniment" of mental with physical events, and so we must now ask whether, if he was indeed a parallelist of the epiphenomenalist variety, Nietzsche had a different theory of causation or simply failed to see all of the logical connections involved. That he failed to see all of the logical connections involved is almost certainly the case (who of us does, after all?), but the situation may well point more interestingly to what he thought about the nature of causation itself. My suggestion is that, even though his basic view of causation would have allowed him to be a parallelist without being an epiphenomenalist, he simply did not recognize this possibility.

For now, however, I propose to postpone my discussion of Nietzsche on causation to the next chapter and, before turning to some of the literature to examine how others have regarded Nietzsche's views on the connection of mind and body, to say something about the notion of the unconscious and Nietzsche's views on it.

The notion of the unconscious naturally turns the mind to Sigmund Freud, and it is well known that he had a great admiration for Nietzsche while claiming that he was unable to read him (or any philosopher). Freud did assert that Nietzsche had a greater knowledge of himself than anyone who had ever lived or was likely to live and, coming from him, this would surely have involved the notion of the unconscious. He may have been aware of, and would surely have admired, Nietzsche's maxim that "One's own self is well hidden from oneself: of all mines of treasure one's own is the last to be dug up." At the same time, the widely-believed claim that Freud in any significant way derived his ideas about the unconscious from Nietzsche is almost certainly false. But it is equally false, though not so widely-believed, that the idea of the unconscious originates with Freud. But nor does it originate with Nietzsche.

Nietzsche, in a passage in *The Gay Science*, appears to ascribe the origin of the unconscious to Gottfried Leibniz:

> First, *Leibniz's* incomparable insight that has been vindicated not only against Descartes but against everybody who had philosophized before him—that consciousness is merely an *accidens* of experience and *not* its necessary and essential attribute; that, in other words, what we call consciousness constitutes only one state of our spiritual and psychic world (perhaps a pathological state) and *not by any means the whole of it*. The profundity of this idea has not been exhausted to this day. (GS 357, Nietzsche's emphases)

And in an earlier entry in the same work, Nietzsche directly asserts the existence and the importance of the unconscious, as well as the distinctly Freudian idea that turmoil in the unconscious can be the source of certain strong feelings in the conscious mind:

> For the longest time, conscious thought was considered thought itself. Only now does the truth dawn on us that by far the greatest part of our spirit's activity remains unconscious and unfelt. But I suppose that these instincts which are here contending against one another understand very well how to make themselves felt by, and how to hurt, *one another*. This may well be the source of that sudden and violent exhaustion that afflicts all thinkers (it is the exhaustion on a battlefield). (GS 333, Nietzsche's emphases)

And in one of the most important passages in Nietzsche, also in *The Gay Science*, on the origin of consciousness (not our present concern), he makes clear that his notion of the unconscious is not that merely of dispositional mental states:

> The problem of consciousness (more precisely, of becoming conscious of something) confronts us only when we begin to comprehend how we could dispense with it; and now physiology and the history of animals place us at the beginning of such comprehension (it took them two centuries to catch up with *Leibniz's* suspicion which soared ahead). For we could think, feel, will, and remember, and we could also "act" in every sense of that word, and yet none of this would have to "enter our consciousness" (as one says metaphorically). The whole of life would be possible without, as it were, seeing itself in a mirror. Even now, for that matter, by far the greatest portion of our life actually takes place without this mirror effect; and this is true even of our thinking, feeling, and willing life, however offensive this may sound to older philosophers. (GS 354, Nietzsche's emphasis)

We have several questions before us. What is the unconscious, ontologically speaking? What is Nietzsche's notion of the unconscious? How does the notion fit with what I have already said about his ontology of mind?

(And was Richard Rorty, in his *Philosophy and the Mirror of Nature*, aware of Nietzsche's characterization of the conscious mind as a "mirror"?)

At the beginning of this chapter, I briefly reiterated my longstanding view that the mind is best understood under the heading of three categories: conscious mental states (making up the stream of consciousness), entities that depend on conscious mental states for their existence without being constituents of them, and dispositional mental states. On the face of it, these categories seem to provide no room for the notion of the unconscious. My reply to this worry is to say that unconscious mental states are comprised of a subset of conscious mental states and a subset of dispositional mental states. This will need some explaining.

Saying that some unconscious mental states are a subset of conscious mental states jars, but the terminological awkwardness is easily overcome. By a conscious mental state, I mean a state that, unlike a purely dispositional mental state (which, as we speak, a person can have in dreamless sleep or under full anesthesia), actually involves awareness. But such awarenesses occur with different degrees of intensity and—what is not quite the same thing—different levels of accessibility by what we might call the fully conscious mind. Two examples will illustrate both aspects. As I sit at the computer writing these words, I have had the wall behind the computer in my visual field, I have had the pressure of the chair on my body in my kinesthetic field, and I have had noises in the hallway in my auditory field. In no case was I paying attention, as one might say, to what was in these fields but, in each case, I can, as I now have, become fully aware of the objects of these awarenesses and also cognizant of the fact that, at some level, I was aware of them all along. The other example is that of blindsight, the phenomenon of being able to see without being able to bring such visual awareness to the conscious mind, a phenomenon due usually to stroke or other damage to the brain. Some people with blindsight vehemently deny that they can see at any level of awareness, but that they can see is far and away the best explanation of certain of their abilities.

With these two examples we can distinguish cases in which the kind of awareness a person had earlier can easily become a full awareness from cases in which the kind of awareness a person had cannot be brought to full or any degree of, *in one sense of the word*, conscious awareness. Still, it is a kind of *awareness* and not merely a dispositional mental state, and so, *in another sense of the word*, is a conscious mental state. More generally, we may suppose that there is a continuum, in all the forms of awareness from those that are, at a moment, those of full consciousness to those that are inaccessible altogether, for whatever reason, to full consciousness, except by way of simply thinking about them. Those toward that end of accessibility, either absolutely or only with difficulty (for example, by psychoanalysis) are what constitute the more interesting part of what, historically speaking anyway, has been considered the realm of the unconscious.

The other part, I said, is that of a subset of dispositional mental states. I doubt that Nietzsche any more than Freud ever made a systematic distinction, in word or thought, between these ontologically very different kinds of unconscious mental states; and while both clearly are thinking more often and more interestingly of the part of the unconscious that is a form of actual awareness discussed above (for example, in his list of thinking, feeling, willing, and remembering in the quote above), Nietzsche often regards the instincts (as in another of the quotes above) as being, or being a part of, the unconscious. And while instincts may express themselves in conscious mental states of any kind or level of awareness, they themselves should, whatever Nietzsche may have thought, be regarded as dispositional mental states—dispositions, that is, to have both certain conscious mental states and behaviors, under certain conditions.

Thus do I accommodate the notion of the unconscious within the categories I originally set out for understanding the general notion of mind or the mental, in the ontological sense. And I say unhesitatingly that the unconscious certainly exists, in both aspects I have described, without necessarily subscribing to either the specific contents or the causal roles that either Nietzsche or Freud ascribed to them. Whatever exactly his influence on Freud was, Nietzsche greatly advanced the importance of the notion of the unconscious, possibly giving it an even exaggerated role in the explanation of behavior. But here my task was not to attempt to say just what the role is for Nietzsche, but only to understand its general nature and importance in his thought.

As a final observation: I can well imagine that Nietzsche would be sympathetic with an ontological account of dispositions, whether mental or behavioral only, that regards them as states of the brain (in us anyway) as subject to certain laws. Such a brain state is what is sometimes known as the "ground" of a disposition, much as the molecular structure of sugar is the ground of its disposition to dissolve in water. Locating our dispositional mental states in our physiology directly would surely draw Nietzsche's approval.

With that I am ready to turn to the literature. Even considering only that part of the vast literature on Nietzsche that explicitly considers his ontology of mind, including its relation to the body, almost none of it has any discussion of the sort I have engaged in and, therefore, any ascription of any specific ontology to him. Two exceptions are to be found in Peter Poellner's *Nietzsche and Metaphysics* and Richard Schacht's *Nietzsche*, which I shall examine in that order.

Poellner's discussion of Nietzsche and the unconscious is the most detailed and the most valuable that I have found in the literature, including his assembly of the relevant texts from Nietzsche. It is focused on the assumption that, for Nietzsche, "the efficacious antecedents of human behavior—both 'voluntary' and 'involuntary'—are not to be discovered in consciousness, i.e. they are *unconscious*." (1995, 213, Poellner's emphasis). Accordingly, in a section entitled 'Unconscious Mental States', he devotes about sixteen pages to a discussion of the notion itself and Nietzsche's involvement with it. Poellner may move a little too quickly, as the quote suggests, from the claim that, if the causes of behavior are not conscious mental states, then they are unconscious mental states (unless the latter were a catch-all expression), for Nietzsche often suggests that the causes of some behavioral and conscious mental states are just brute physiological states; that is, neither unconscious mental states (including dispositional mental states) nor conscious mental states but states like indigestion, for example. Further, the thesis that there are unconscious mental states and that they have a causal role in the explanation of both behavior and conscious mental states does not require the thesis that conscious mental states are "mere" epiphenomena. Freud understood that very well or, better said, he took it entirely for granted, never doubting the efficacy of conscious mental states while at the same time insisting on the existence and efficacy of unconscious mental states.

Poellner rightly emphasizes the ambiguity of many of the relevant texts, calling attention to Nietzsche's highly intentionalistic language in talking about the unconscious, even when it seems to be understood as dispositions (1995, 216). Indeed, Poellner appears to be skeptical of the coherence of the notion of unconscious mental states conceived as occurrent, intentional states. I have already given reasons—examples, if you like—for believing in something of that sort; and one wonders what Poellner and other critics of the idea of occurrent, unconscious mental states make of the phenomenon of blindsight, for example. But it is only fair to say that he is especially concerned with Nietzsche's emphasis on desiring, will, and thinking as unconscious; and it may be thought (but not by me) that these notions do not so easily admit of admission to the postulated realm of occurrent unconscious mental states, as I have characterized them.

A further focus of Poellner's discussion, a matter that I have ignored but one that is obviously important to Nietzsche's discussion of the unconscious, is that of self-deception, especially in connection with the will to power as it occurs in human beings. The theme of self-deception is a common one in the so-called existentialist philosophers and one reason, among many to the contrary, for so classifying Nietzsche. I have ignored this aspect of Nietzsche's thought because it is not ontological. The theory of the will to power, which is ontological, I will discuss later, although with little connection to his ontology of mind.

Quoting an interesting note of 1887 (WP 479), Poellner remarks that Nietzsche does sometimes allow, after all, that we have, or at least may have, direct access to some of the contents of consciousness. Nietzsche writes (and here I quote more of the note than Poellner does):

> "Inner experience" enters our consciousness only after it has found a language the individual understands—i.e., a translation of a condition into conditions familiar to him--; "to understand" means merely: to be able to express something new in the language of something old and familiar. E.g., "I feel unwell"—such a judgment presupposes a great and late neutrality of the observer--; the simple man always says: this or that makes me feel unwell only when he has seen a reason for feeling unwell.-- I call that a *lack of philology*; to be able to read off a text as a text without interposing an interpretation is the last-developed form of "inner experience"—perhaps one that is hardly possible-- (KGW VIII 15 [90], Nietzsche's emphasis)

I have already maintained that Nietzsche, like every other philosopher and every other human being, does and must presuppose the existence of a mind-independent reality of which we have some knowledge. This in turn presupposes, not that we *do* have direct access to, and some knowledge of, our own minds, but that, *if* we do introspect and therefore attend to what is there, we *can* have such knowledge. In particular, we can of knowledge of what it is we are thinking about—not knowledge of the object of the thought, but of the fact that one is thinking about such-and-such an object and not something else or nothing at all. For example, as I sit here and write, I know that it is Nietzsche that I am thinking about. And when Nietzsche or anyone else says, as some causal theorists of the mind and others do say, that we may not even know what the content (neutral sense) of our present thought is, he and they are presupposing the precise opposite as they speak and write. This, again, is perhaps the most radical case of presupposing the falsity of skepticism in attempting to make an argument for skepticism.

One finds also in this passage a point similar to one that I have argued (1989, 60-65): that the ability to make sense of one's own mind may depend on having a language. For me this is a causal dependence only, while for others—Sellars, for example—somehow the nature of awareness itself is ontologically bound up with language. It is unclear what Nietzsche's view is, or would be if the issue were posed to him, on this matter. But there is also a hint of the somewhat different thesis, associated with Wittgenstein, that, at least initially, conscious states can be understood only by way of aspects of the public world, mainly perhaps as whatever it is in me that is caused by, or causes, this or that public occurrence. But, as with Wittgenstein, this idea is more hinted at than developed in any systematic way. The crucial fact, as I see it, is that, whatever role language plays in our ability to become aware of our own minds and to whatever extent "[a]n 'inner process' stands in need of outward criteria" (Wittgenstein, 1953, sec. 580), we obviously do come to be able to recognize and describe much of our inner life, whatever some philosophers may say or suggest to the contrary. If that were not so then, as I suggested above, no sense could be made of what I am doing as I write these words and what you are doing when you read them. This is not to say that the mind, not even the conscious mind, is wholly transparent or that we cannot err in our beliefs and descriptions of what is there even at the moment of its occurrence, but only that, in philosophy as in all intellectual endeavors and much more, we necessarily presuppose, what very much seems to be the case anyway, that for the most part what seems to be going on in our minds is what is going on in our minds. And I can't help but think that Nietzsche, on reflection, would agree.

In his *Nietzsche*, Richard Schacht sees Nietzsche's philosophy of mind in somewhat similar but still importantly different ways from the views I have put forward above. In general, Schacht is inclined to ascribe less extreme positions to Nietzsche than I have; and with respect especially to what I see as his epiphenomalism, Schacht writes:

> A balanced and careful consideration of his discussion of consciousness shows, therefore, that he is no more a true epiphenomenalist than he is a strict determinist. The occasional remarks he makes which are suggestive of the former position may both reasonably and most coherently be interpreted as somewhat overstated reactions on his part against the attribution of causality to certain sorts of conscious events in the explanation of human actions. He is in effect exclaiming: 'Causalism indeed! Epiphenomenalism is closer to the mark!' Once the former doctrine is disposed of, however, the occasion for the employment of such strong contrasting language as a needed corrective passes as well. And when one looks beyond it, one can see that the view he is actually advancing is somewhat less extreme, even though still quite radical in relation to traditional philosophical (and religious) thought. (1992, 314-315)

Perhaps. After citing some texts that seem to support the attribution of epiphenomenalism to Nietzsche, Schacht cites others--WP 671, GS 360, WP 676, GS 335--that, he thinks, support the weaker position he ascribes to him. So let us have a look at those texts, always granting that, like so much in Nietzsche and especially in his notes to himself, we are dealing with a thinker in action, so to speak. The whole of the note of 1883-84 (WP 671) reads as follows:

> Freedom of the will or no freedom of the will?-- There is no such thing as "will"; it is only a simplifying conception of understanding, as is "matter."
> All actions must first be made possible mechanically before they are willed. Or the "purpose" *usually* comes into the mind only after everything has been prepared for its execution. The end is an "inner" "stimulus"—no more. (KGW VII 24 [32-34], Nietzsche's emphasis)

Schacht thinks that Nietzsche's referring to the purpose as a stimulus, even though both words are set off with double quotes, indicates some causal role for what is in consciousness. I would be more inclined to read it, especially because of the double quotes, to mean something more like: that aspect of consciousness that is mistakenly taken to be a stimulus (without double quotes). (His double-quoting of 'inner' is, I take it, a recognition that it is spatial metaphor.)

In this same connection, Schacht refers us to *The Gay Science*, from which he quotes parts of the following sentences:

> This seems to me to be one of my most essential steps and advances: I have learned to distinguish the cause of acting from the cause of acting in a particular way, in a particular direction, with a particular goal. . . . People are accustomed to consider the goal (purposes, vocations, etc.) as the *driving force*, in keeping with a very ancient error, but it is merely the *directing* force—one has mistaken the helmsman for the steam. And not even always the helmsman, the directing force. (GS 360, Nietzsche's emphases)

Before I comment on these important sentences, I note that in the same entry, immediately following the last sentence just quoted, Nietzsche says the following:

> Is the "goal," the "purpose" not often enough a beautifying pretext, a self-deception of vanity after the event that does not want to acknowledge that the ship is *following* the current into which it has entered accidentally? that it "wills" to go that way *because it—must*? that it has a direction, to be sure, but—no helmsman at all?
> We still need a critique of the concept of "purpose." (GS 360, Nietzsche's emphases)

Schacht might well call attention in this passage to the phrase 'not often enough' as again leaving open some role, sometimes, for the conscious purpose to be the determining in why a person did this and not that, and perhaps he would be right to do so. In fact, I think he would be right, *in a sense*. But before I have my fuller say, let us look briefly at the other passages he refers us to in this context. In a note of 1883-84 (WP 676), Nietzsche writes:

> Formerly, one explained the motions of the stars as effects produced by entities conscious of a purpose. One no longer needs this explanation, and in regard to bodily motions and changes, too, one has long since abandoned the belief in an explanation by means of a consciousness that determines purposes. By far the greater number of motions have nothing whatever to do with consciousness; nor with sensation. Sensations and thoughts are something extremely insignificant

and rare in relation to the countless number of events that occur at every moment. (KGW VII 24 [16])

Here, as elsewhere, Nietzsche seems to state unequivocally the inefficacy of conscious states in the explanation of behavior. But where Schacht sees the last two sentences as indicating that, while "the far greater number" of behaviors are not affected by consciousness, some are so affected, I read it as saying only that most behaviors ("events") are not even *accompanied* by consciousness or sensations, much less (even partially) *caused* by them; some are so accompanied and most not by consciousness, but none caused but it.

In the fourth of the passages that Schacht cites in this immediate context, in *The Gay Science*, Nietzsche's concern is to reject what we would now call intuitionism in ethics or any theory that relies in appeal to one's "conscience" or to a perceived "categorical imperative". For the point I want to make, it will be worthwhile quoting the entire (very long) sentence in which the parts that Schacht quotes occur, as well as the immediately preceding sentence:

> Anyone who still judges "in this case everybody would have to act like this" has not yet taken five steps toward self-knowledge. Otherwise, he would know that there neither are nor can be actions that are the same; that every action that has ever been done was done in an altogether unique and irretrievable way; and that this will be equally true of every future action; that all regulations about actions relate only to their coarse exterior (even the most inward and subtle regulations of all moralities so far); that these regulations may lead to some semblance of sameness, *but really only to some semblance*; that as one contemplates or looks back upon *any* action at all, it is and remains impenetrable; that our opinions about "good" and "noble" and "great" can never be *proved true* by our actions because every action is unknowable; that our opinions, valuations, and tables of what is good certainly belong among the most powerful levers in the involved mechanism of our actions, but that in any particular case the law of their mechanism is indemonstrable. (GS 335, Nietzsche's emphases)

Schacht takes the last few lines of this passage to indicate that our values are being said to have causal efficacy with respect to our actions and, therefore, more evidence that Nietzsche should not be taken to be a "true epiphenomenalist".

I begin by putting aside what I take to be the fact that what Nietzsche calls "opinions, valuations, and tables of what is good" are not conscious mental states or even aspects of them, but instead are dispositional mental states. If that is so, then they are not, strictly speaking, relevant to the issue of epiphenomenalism, which pertains only to conscious mental states. (The failure systematically to distinguish dispositional from conscious mental states, which is essential to the issues of epiphenomenalism and parallelism, almost wholly destroys the argument of Donald Davidson in his well-known "Mental Events" against the possibility of strict psychophysical laws, or so I claim.)

But let us assume either that the mental things Nietzsche mentions really are aspects of conscious mental states or that he could instead have mentioned things that in fact are aspects of conscious mental states. The point I want to make begins by stressing that the focus of this passage, like that of the entire entry, is not at all on any theory about the role of consciousness in the explanation of behavior but instead, as already indicated, on matters of moral philosophy. It is a long entry, the part quoted constituting about one sixth of the whole. Like everyone, philosopher or not, and, if philosopher, whatever theory he or she may hold about the connection of mind and body, Nietzsche frequently speaks commonsensically about mental things as having an explanatory role in the occurrence of behavior. Even the kind of materialist who denies that there is such a thing as the mind or consciousness will attribute the behavior, one's own or someone else's, of, for example, eating rapidly after long deprivation to the desire to get rid of one's hunger, or turning around on the way home from work to suddenly remembering that one was charged with getting food for supper. I believe that good philosophy should, as far as possible, accommodate the commonsense view of reality including the apparent facts of the existence and efficacy of consciousness. But I do not regard everyday mentalistic explanations of behavior by philosophers who, as philosophers, deny the efficacy or even the existence of consciousness as evidence that they do not in fact hold those views. Or, perhaps better said, while I might say that it is not really possible for anyone to believe some of these theories about the existence and efficacy of consciousness, the fact that they engage in everyday mentalistic explanations is not evidence against the thesis that, when the issues of such existence and efficacy are at hand, their texts do not really mean what they seem to mean.

This is a situation, as occurs so often in dealing with Nietzsche in which it pays to give strict attention to what the main issue under discussion is. As we saw in the matter of whether or not Nietzsche is an idealist, even though there are some texts that could be understood in that way, whenever idealism is itself the topic at hand, Nietzsche rejects it. So with epiphenomenalism, I believe, although, of course, the label is not always used in the discussion. And this, probably, is as far as we can go. What Nietzsche *really* believed is probably impossible to know, but also not really very important. I have argued that the texts, especially when one applies the conditions I have indicated, support taking Nietzsche, as philosopher and writer, as an epiphenomenalist and a parallelist. I also argued that one can even agree with the heart of what Nietzsche "wants" to say, and still maintain the truth of at least some attributions of efficacy to conscious mental states in the explanation of behavior. That, we saw, depends on the theory of causation that one, implicitly or explicitly, holds to be true.

Thus, to Nietzsche on causation we know turn.

CAUSATION

Sometimes Nietzsche sees causality everywhere; sometimes he can't find it anywhere. But these are not simply the projections of the sober Nietzsche and the wild Nietzsche, respectively. It is much more complicated than that. Although Nietzsche often denies that there is any such thing as a cause, he often also contrasts real causes with fictional or imaginary causes and chastises those who reverse cause and effect, obviously assuming that there are genuine cases of something causing something else. What is going on here? Can one really construct anything like a consistent view of causation in Nietzsche's writings?

The place where Nietzsche writes most about causation (or what he usually calls, at least in translation, 'causality') is in *The Will to Power*; indeed, far more there than in everything else put together. But it is for the most part consistent with what he says in the writings he published while going into much more detail than any of the latter. As we know, the notes are often, even in their written form, more musings, wonderings, questionings than affirmations. But in the many passages in *The Will to Power* that deal with causation, there is a strong verbal consistency. I say 'verbal' because one may wonder if there is really a consistency of content or indeed even a full intelligibility. I shall argue that, once one gets by what, for later analytic philosophers, is a confusing and eccentric terminology, one can find a consistent and even somewhat plausible theory of causation in Nietzsche.

My view is that Nietzsche has a Humean view of causation, somewhat despite himself and even his explicit, apparent rejection of it. But let us begin with a passage from *The Will to Power* in which it is obvious that Nietzsche is familiar with Hume's views on causation even if, possibly, he doesn't entirely grasp their full ontological implications. In an entry dated 1885-1886 (WP 550), Nietzsche writes:

> The question "why?" is always a question after the *causa finalis,* after the "what for?" We have no "sense for the *causa efficiens*": here Hume was right; habit (but not only that of the individual!) makes us expect that a certain often-observed occurrence will follow another: nothing more! That which gives the

> extraordinary firmness to our belief in causality is not the great habit of seeing one occurrence following another but our inability to interpret events otherwise than as events caused by intentions. It is belief in the living and thinking as the only effective force—in will, in intention—it is belief that every event is a deed, that every deed presupposes a doer, it is belief in the "subject." Is this belief in the concept of subject and attribute not a great stupidity?
> Question: is intention the cause of an event? Or is that also illusion.
> Is it not the event itself? (KGW VIII 2 [83])

There is much more in this passage than the agreement with Hume on a crucial point. And I shall attend to that momentarily. But let us first fix firmly in our minds Nietzsche's agreement with Hume on that crucial point: that we have no experience of an entity that might be called, if it existed, the causal connection of some particular event to some other particular event. There is not event A and event B *and* the causal connection between them when we are in a perceptual situation that leads us to believe that A caused B. Thus our basis, both psychological and ontological, for maintaining that A caused B must lie elsewhere. Or, perhaps, there is no such basis; that the whole idea of causation is illusion. It is in this difference between saying that the ontological basis of causation lies elsewhere and saying that the idea of causation is fictitious that Nietzsche straddles, so to speak–sometimes leaning in one direction and sometimes in the other. This is what I hope to establish, from text and argument.

But let us be clear on a general matter: the real question before the philosopher on causation should be, not whether or not there is such a thing as causation, but instead that of its ontology. Some philosophers are inclined to hold that if one denies that there is an entity that is present in the particular case, then one is holding that there is no such thing as causation. This is similar to the thesis that if one denies that the self is a substance, then one is holding that there are no selves; or, more generally, that if one denies there that there are substances, then one is holding that there are no things. (Nietzsche, we saw, is a victim of the last-mention conflation.) In all cases, one should start with the commonsense world of causation, selves, and things and ask, once more, not of their existence but of their ontology. Like everyone, Nietzsche in practice, as one says, of course holds to the existence of causation, selves, and things; but, like some philosophers, he sometimes also denies their existence. As we may now suspect, what he is really denying is a certain ontological analysis, in each case.

With these thoughts in mind, let us first consider the sober Nietzsche who not only recognizes causation in the everyday world, but writes about it in many ordinary cases in order to attack religion or established morality or other points of view. Indeed, in *The Genealogy of Morals,* in the context of his account of "breeding" an animal "with the right to make promises" in the broader context of what is presupposed by the idea of morality, Nietzsche writes:

> To ordain the future in advance in this way, man must first have learned to distinguish necessary events from chance ones, to think causally, to see and anticipate distant eventualities as if they belonged to the present, to decide with certainty what is the goal and what the means to it, and in general be able to calculate and compute. Man himself must first of all have become *calculable, regular, necessary*, even in his own image of himself, if he is to be able to stand security for *his own future*, which is what one who promises does! (GM II 1, Nietzsche's emphases)

Here we are told that to be able to think causally is of the essence of being (or becoming) human. The very idea of planning what one is going to do presupposes causal thought and a world of regular causal connections. Here, of course, the ontology of causation is not at all at issue, nor should it be. It is entirely taken for granted by Nietzsche that there are causal connections and that we can know some of them.

In a passage from which I earlier quoted in *The Gay Science*, Nietzsche writes freely of general and particular causes, and their role in the explanation of human behavior. Here it is worth quoting at some length:

> *Two kinds of causes that are often confounded.*—This seems to me to be one of my most essential steps and advances: I have learned to distinguish the cause of acting from the cause of acting in a particular way, in a particular direction, with a particular goal. The first kind of cause is a quantum of dammed-up energy that is waiting to be used up somehow, for something, while the second kind is, compared to this energy, something quite insignificant, for the most part a little accident in accordance with which this quantum "discharges" itself in one particular way–a match versus a ton of powder. Among these little accidents and "matches" I include so-called "purposes" as well as the even much more so-called "vocations": They are relatively random, arbitrary, almost indifferent in relation to the tremendous quantum of energy that presses, as I have said, to be used up somehow. The usual view is different: People are accustomed to consider the goal (purposes, vocations, etc.) as the *driving force,* in

> keeping with a very ancient error; but it is merely the *directing* force–one has mistaken the helmsman for the steam. And not even always the helmsman, the directing force. (GS 360, Nietzsche's emphases)

As we saw, this is a passage that Schacht reasonably cites in support of his view that Nietzsche is not a full-blown epiphenomenalist. About that matter, I had my say in the last chapter. The distinction Nietzsche makes in the passage is, or ought to be, a thoroughly familiar one to us, expressed in many ways, but in one as that between standing conditions (or causes) and changing conditions (or causes). For a less controversial but similar example: the presence of oxygen, being necessary for me to be conscious, makes it possible for me to choose what to do this evening. But what I do in particular is the result of the particular choice I make.

In *The Twilight of the Idols,* Nietzsche writes at some length of causes in a way that obviously presupposes a world of causes, some of which can be known and, indeed, are claimed to be known by him in his critique of religion and morality. The most important passage is the section called "The Four Great Errors" even though some sentences in it are sometimes cited (for example, by Schacht) to document Nietzsche's skepticism about causation's even existing. Clearly, the overall thrust of the passage takes causation for granted even only in considering the names of the errors: the error of confusing cause and effect, the error of a false causality, the error of imaginary causes, the error of free will. Let us briefly consider each.

With respect to the error of confusing cause and effect, Nietzsche cites the simple (and not very convincing) example of a diet book by someone named Cornaro, who claimed that his diet was the cause of his good health and long life. Nietzsche, to the contrary, says that his good health was the cause of his diet. More interesting is Nietzsche's claim that, contrary to religion and morality, which teach that the way to happiness is to be virtuous, ". . . virtue is the *effect* of . . . happiness", at least in the "well-turned out human being." (TI "The Four Great Errors" 2, Nietzsche's emphasis)

The error of a false causality is more complicated and perhaps somewhat confused. I cited much of the relevant passage earlier in my discussion of Nietzsche's ontology of mind, in support of my attribution to him of epiphenomenalism. He does seem at first to be attacking the very notion of causality; the first sentence reads "People have believed at all times that they knew what a cause is . . ." and goes on, apparently challenging this belief. But his initial conclusion is only, as we saw earlier, that "There are no mental causes at all." And his more general conclusion is, not that there are no causes of what happens, but that what happens is not the effect of willing–ours or anything else's–"The error of the spirit as cause mistaken for reality!" (TI "The Four Great Errors 3).

Concerning the error of imaginary causes, Nietzsche first cites the case of dreams, but then turns to the question of the causes of good and bad feelings. Here again, far from denying that there are causes, he refers to their real causes (as well as offering a causal explanation of why we do not get at the real causes):

> Memory, which swings into action in such cases, unknown to us, brings up earlier states of the same kind, together with the causal interpretations associated with them–not their real causes. The faith, to be sure, that such representations, such accompanying conscious processes, are the causes, is also brought forth by memory. Thus originates a habitual acceptance of a particular causal interpretation, which, as a matter of fact, inhibits any investigation into the real cause– even precludes it. (TI "The Four Great Errors" 4)

He proceeds in the next section to give his more general "psychological explanation" of this phenomenon, itself a causal explanation, and goes on in the succeeding section to claim that *"The whole realm of morality and religion belongs under this concept of imaginary causes"* (Nietzsche's emphases) and concludes the passage by this summary of the first three errors with respect to religion and morality:

> Morality and religion belong altogether to the *psychology of error*: in every single case, cause and effect are confused; or truth is confused with the effects of *believing* something to be true; or a state of consciousness is confused with its causes. (TI "The Four Great Errors" 6, Nietzsche's emphases)

The fourth "great" error, that of free will, is less relevant to my aim of demonstrating how committed Nietzsche really is to a world of causation. The main point of the passage, denying again that our wills, caused or not, are themselves the causes of our actions is clear. In denying free will, Nietzsche is obviously at odds with most or all of the other members of that group of thinkers with which he is often classified–the existentialists. Yet, in saying that "no one *gives* man his qualities–neither God, nor society, nor his parents and ancestors, nor he himself" and that "No one is responsible for man's being there at all, for his being such-and-such, or for his being in these circumstances or in this environment" (TI "The Four Great Errors" 8, Nietzsche's emphasis), he comes close to the atheistic existentialism of Jean-Paul Sartre. But his further claim that "One is necessary, one is a piece of fatefulness, one belongs to the whole, one is in the whole" in the same passage sounds like a commitment to a full determinism (as do other passages, at least one of which I shall cite later). And determinism makes no sense apart from a commitment to causation or, at least, to regularity.

But this last point invites us to take a closer look at the related notions of causation, regularity, lawfulness, necessity, and calculability. Sorting out what is involved in each and what Nietzsche has to say about each will, if I am not mistaken, bring us to a much clearer understanding of what Nietzsche took the world to be like in the respect under discussion, the ontology of causation. But first (although the matters are intertwined) we must consider Nietzsche's frequent attacks on the notion and reality of causation, mostly in *The Will to Power*, but also occasionally in his writings intended for publication.

Turning again to *The Gay Science*, we find a passage which is, in general, written against the idea that the world has either internal or external purpose, with the following words:

> The total character of the world, however, is in all eternity chaos–in the sense not of a lack of necessity but of a lack of order, arrangement, form, beauty, wisdom, and whatever other names there are for our aesthetic anthropomorphisms. . . . Let us beware of saying that there are laws in nature. There are only necessities: there is nobody who commands, nobody who obeys, nobody who trespasses. (GS 109)

Here Nietzsche affirms necessity in nature, but denies lawfulness, apparently still in the grasp of the notion of a law of nature in medieval thought, even though philosophers since then had long separated that notion from that of something or someone who commands, as well as that of so-called "natural law"–rights and obligations said to be somehow written into the very fabric of nature. Spinoza, for example (and someone whom Nietzsche admired greatly), is very clear that while the universe is wholly law-bound, this has nothing to do with either commands or morality.

In *Beyond Good and Evil*, Nietzsche sounds a theme that becomes stronger in *The Will to Power,* murky as the passage is:

> One should not wrongly reify "cause" and "effect," as the natural scientists do (and whoever, like them, now "naturalizes" in his thinking), according to the prevailing mechanical doltishness which makes the cause press and push until it "effects" its end; one should use "cause" and "effect" only as pure concepts, that is to say, as conventional fictions for the purpose of designation and communication–*not* for explanation. In the "in-itself" there is nothing of "causal connections," of "necessity," or of "psychological non-freedom"; there the effect does *not* follow the cause, there is no rule of "law." It is *we* alone who have devised cause, sequence, for-each-other, relativity, constraint, number, law, freedom, motive, and purpose; and when we project and mix this symbol world into things as if it existed "in itself," we act once more as we have always acted—*mythologically.* The "unfree will" is mythology; it real life it is only a matter of *strong* and *weak* wills. (BGE 21, Nietzsche's emphases)

And in the next section, Nietzsche again, somewhat mysteriously, contrasts being "necessary" and "calculable" with "conformity to law" in the context of a broader contrast between an "interpretation" of the phenomena as lawful and regarding them as the result of the "will to power." Addressing the physicists, he writes:

> *Ni Dieu, ni maître* [Neither God nor master]–that is what you, too, want; and therefore "cheers for the law of nature!"–is it not so? But . . . that is interpretation, not text; and somebody might come along who, with opposite intentions and modes of interpretation, could read out of the same "nature," and with regard to the same phenomena, rather the tyrannically inconsiderate and relentless enforcement of claims of power–an interpreter who would picture the unexceptional and unconditional aspects of all "will to power" so vividly that almost every word, even the word "tyranny" itself, would eventually seem unsuitable, or a weakening and attenuating metaphor–being too human–but he might, nevertheless, end by asserting the same about this world as you do, namely, that it has a "necessary" and "calculable" course, *not* because laws obtain in it, but because they are absolutely *lacking*, and every power draws its ultimate consequence at every moment. (BGE 22, Nietzsche's emphases)

We may also note about this passage that Nietzsche seems to assume, and be entirely comfortable with the assumption, that the phenomena are, as it were, given and neutral, so to speak, with their explanation, however, being a matter of "interpretation."

Finally, from the same work, I take note of a well-known passage in which Nietzsche contrasts his theory (though here tentatively advanced) of the will to power with any theory of multiple kinds of causes, apparently taking for granted the objective reality of causation in nature. The passage has its confusing aspects–for example, seeming both to affirm and to deny that the will can act on matter and also, perhaps (a matter for later discussion), confusing the ordinary human will with the will to power:

> In the end not only is it permitted to make this experiment: the conscience of *method* demands it. Not to assume several kinds of causality until the experiment of making do with a single one has been pushed to it utmost limit... The question is in the end whether we really recognize the will as *efficient*, whether we believe in the causality of the will: if we do–and at bottom our faith in this is nothing less than our faith in causality itself–then we have to make the experiment of positing the causality of the will hypothetically as the only one. "Will," of course, can affect only "will"—and not "matter" (not "nerves," for example). In short, one has to risk the hypothesis whether will does not affect will wherever "effects" are recognized–and whether all mechanical occurrences are not, insofar as a force is active in them, will force, effects of will.
>
> Suppose, finally, we succeeded in explaining our entire instinctive life as the development and ramification of *one* basic form of the will–namely, of the will to power, as *my* proposition has it; suppose all organic functions could be traced back to this will to power and one could also find in it the solution of the problem of procreation and nourishment–it is *one* problem–then one would have gained the right to determine *all* efficient force univocally as–*will to power*. (BGE 36, Nietzsche's emphases)

Here, then, we have causes, or *a* cause, but not laws. What he might mean by this becomes somewhat clearer in some of his notes, which, as we have already observed, contain the great majority of Nietzsche's written comments on causation. But let us start with a note of the sober Nietzsche, dated spring 1888 (WP 136), in which he ascribes a certain defect to the religious person:

> *Rudimentary psychology of the religious man*:— All changes are effects; all effects are effects of will (—the concept "nature," "law of nature" is lacking); all effects suppose an agent. (KGW VIII 14 [125], Nietzsche's emphases)

Here, it seems, having the "concept" of a law of nature and, presumably, taking their existence for a fact is a virtue, but one not to be found in the religious person. Still, as we shall see, the overall thrust of the many passages on causation in *The Will to Power* is to deny, at least in words, that there are laws of nature. I put it that way because, as I have already suggested, many of those same passages and same words can be said to support the existence of laws of nature on Nietzsche's part, not, perhaps, as Nietzsche conceived them, but as we now would, or well might, conceive them. This is, I further suggest, a clear case in which we must look at, and then through, Nietzsche's words in order to say how he actually took reality to be. Let us see.

Arguably, the most important passage on causality in all of Nietzsche's so-far published writings is what appears as WP 551. And while, of course, it was not necessarily intended by him for publication, it has the force of having been written in spring 1888, near the end of his thinking life. So I will quote large parts of it:

> *Critique of the concept "cause"*— We have absolutely no experience of a cause; psychologically considered, we derive the entire concept from the subjective conviction that *we* are causes, namely, that the arm moves— But that is an error. We separate ourselves, the doers, from the deed, and we make use of this pattern everywhere–we seek a doer for every event. . . .
> There is no such thing as "cause"; some cases in which it seemed to be given to us, and in which we have projected it out of ourselves in order to understand an event, have been shown to be self-deceptions. Our "understanding of an event" has consisted in our inventing a subject which was made responsible for something that happens and for how it happens. We have combined our feeling of will, our feeling of "freedom," our feeling of responsibility and our intention to perform an act, into the concept "cause": *causa efficiens* and *causa finalis* are fundamentally one.
> . . .
> A necessary sequence of states does not imply a causal relationship between them . . . There are neither causes nor effects. Linguistically we do not know how to rid ourselves of them. But that does not matter. . . .
> *In summa*: an event is neither effected nor does it effect. *Causa* is a capacity to produce effects that has been super-added to the events—
> . . . In fact science has emptied the concept causality of its content and retained it as a formula of an equation, in which it has become at bottom a matter of indifference on which side cause is placed and on which side effect. . . . The *calculability of an event* does not reside in the fact that a rule is adhered to, or that a necessity is obeyed, or that a law of causality had been projected by us into every event: it resides in the *recurrence of "identical cases."* (KGW VIII 14 [98])

Most of the crucial terms and themes that pervade Nietzsche's discussion of causality in *The Will to Power* occur in this passage. A few others do not. The crucial terms are 'necessity', calculability', 'regularity', 'recurrence', 'inalterability', 'law of nature', and, of course, 'cause' and its relatives. And there are three broad themes. One comes from the wild Nietzsche to the effect that causality, like much else, is something we project onto a world that is more or less unformed in itself. This is a familiar theme in Nietzsche but, as the reader knows, I have chosen largely to ignore it by regarding it as an expression of Nietzsche at the edge and contrary to so much more that he says, even in the context of his discussion of causality. It is worth noting, however, that it is connected with the thesis of constant change and the supposed consequential non-existence of "things" that we discussed earlier as expressed, for example, in this note of summer 1885 (WP 520):

> Continual transition forbids us to speak of "individuals," etc; the "number" of beings is itself in flux. We would know nothing of time and motion if we did not, in a coarse fashion, believe we see what is at "rest" beside what is in motion. The same applies to cause and effect ... (KGW VII 36 [23])

But this is decidedly a minor aspect of Nietzsche's critique of causation, most of which presupposes that there are discernible events in nature that do stand, and fail to stand, in various relations to each other. So, although this aspect will appear *sotto voce* in at least one other passage I will quote, I have no more to say on this matter.

A second broad theme is that "our" concept of causation is "really" one of agents doing things, that is, of *willing* and *intending* events to occur. Nietzsche is not always consistent on this point, but it is made repeatedly in *The Will to Power* as well as in some of his writings intended for publication, as we have already seen in some of the quotes above. This is related to, but not the same as, the third broad theme: that of distinguishing or separating causation from lawfulness, necessity, regularity, and the like. This is, in my judgment, the most important theme in a discussion of Nietzsche's ontology of causation. Before I turn to that, however, I shall address the second theme.

There is a school of analytic philosophy that regards so-called conceptual analysis as the very heart of correct philosophical method. This is not the place to engage extended discussion of either the nature or importance of this method. But I shall observe, perhaps not quite neutrally, that it seems to presuppose that words have meanings beyond what we recognize them as having, and that those additional, hidden meanings can, at least in principle, be uncovered by this method, also known in some quarters as that of "example/counterexample". If that method is not quite appropriate in the case of Nietzsche's claim about the "concept" of causation, the fact remains that he claims to have uncovered in it an element that, on the face of it, is not there; namely, that to cause is to will. This is *not* the same as saying that the origin of the notion of causation is tied up, somehow, with that of willing. Nor is it the same as saying that in fact, perhaps in some kind of necessary fact as Berkeley maintained, that all cases of causation are cases of willing. It is saying that, in all cases in which we ascribe causation to the connection between two events, we are, *know it or not*, somehow thinking of those events as involving willing or intention or the like.

For some philosophers, myself included, the whole idea that there are hidden meanings of words in the sense required by the method of conceptual analysis is suspect. Considering that huge and mostly uninteresting literature on the "concept" on knowledge in which one proposes to "analyze" the real meaning of 'S knows that P', these philosophers might suggest that the whole enterprise is based on the mistaken assumption that there is something unknown but *discoverable* (if not yet, after thousands of attempts, discover*ed*), but instead only, at most, something to be *decided*. (Nor, I would add for myself, in the case of 'knowledge' does it ever really matter; the far more interesting question is that of rational belief, and which rational beliefs we *decide* to give the honorific 'knowledge' is of little import, philosophically speaking. Furthermore, the *decisions* will vary in many dimensions, according to persons and contexts.)

The import of these reflections with respect to Nietzsche, however, is that one shouldn't try to argue with him about the involvement of causation with willing, as he describes it, except to say either that he is just wrong as a matter of anthropological (linguistic) fact, or that, even if he is correct, there is a recoverable notion of causation (which he himself recognizes and utilizes innumerable times) that is free of the taint of intention. Thus, in this way I reject and dismiss Nietzsche's claim that the "concept" of causation involves willing.

Still, one is not entirely comfortable. For even though Nietzsche had to know that, beginning with Aristotle and the four kinds of causes, through the medievals and their hierarchy of causes, to Spinoza's distinction between transient and immanent causes and much more, philosophers have had notions of causation that seem very much not in any way to involve the notion of willing, he rides his hobby-horse repeatedly, especially in *The Will to Power,* in insisting to the contrary; that, to quote another passage, "The belief in *causae* [efficient causes] falls with the belief in télē [final causes] (against Spinoza and his causalism)" (WP 627, Nietzsche's emphasis). Is it, after all, a case of Nietzsche's falling victim to the philologist's susceptibility to the genetic fallacy? True, Nietzsche, even in this same entry tries, by considering the notions of attraction and repulsion, to tie the notion of causation to that of intention. But this is not so much argument as restatement of the thesis.

I observe again that, like everyone else, Nietzsche invokes and even praises various kinds of causal explanations without any apparent supposition that such explanations involve willing or mind in any way–a supposition, as we know, that would be foreign to some of his deepest convictions about the way things are. So, I ask again, what is going on? My suggestion will lead us to what I called the third theme, and it is this: like some other philosophers, Nietzsche holds that if there is no entity in the particular situation that is the causal connection between the events said to be causally related, then causation does not exist. But what could, in any possible world, such an entity be? It can only be the willing connection, which would, if it existed, exist in the particular situation. But, of course, it does not exist, at least in nearly all of the situations that we ordinarily regard as causal ones. And where there is, in the ordinary sense, willing taking place, there too it is illusion that it is the cause of one's behavior (although, paradoxically, one of his main arguments for this conclusion is that behavior has *other* causes). So, he concludes, causation does not exist.

But if now, in turning to the third theme, we examine how Nietzsche takes the world to be, we shall see that it is a view that many philosophers, and especially philosophers of science and other scientifically-minded philosophers, would regard as one of causality, so to speak, and indeed, one of a full-blown causal determinism. Let us see.

Although one might find some passages that even directly suggest to the contrary, especially in the context of the denial of "things", Nietzsche seems generally to hold, as several of the passages quoted above indicate, that nature is, at least in principle and often in fact, *calculable*, as he puts it. And it is calculable because it is *regular* in its course, as he also puts it. Sometimes, he equates this with necessity in nature; sometimes he denies necessity in nature. In any case, nature is such that we can learn how it goes and so make reliable predictions about its course in some respects, and accommodate our own lives to its inherent regularities. Indeed, as he makes clear in his one interesting argument for the theory of "eternal return" (no good argument is made in *Thus Spoke Zarathustra*, where the theory is discussed, in heavy emotional language, at great length), he is committed to the thesis that *everything* that occurs is part of the regularity of nature, and so, in principle calculable, that is, predictable. That well-known argument occurs in a note of spring 1888 (WP 1066); and, while it is cast in the conditional, it is clear, especially in its attached denial of "a mechanistic conception", that Nietzsche agrees to the antecedent:

> If the world may be thought of as a certain definite quantity of force and a certain definite number of centers of force—and every other representation remains indefinite and therefore useless—it follows that, in the great dice game of existence, it must pass through a calculable number of combinations. In infinite time, every possible combination would at some time or another be realized; more: it would be realized an infinite number of times. And since between every combination and its next recurrence all other possible combinations would have to take place, and each of these combinations conditions the entire sequence of combinations in the same series, a circular movement of absolutely identical series is thus demonstrated: the world as a circular movement that has already repeated itself infinitely often and plays its game *ad infinitum.*
> This conception is not simply a mechanistic conception; for if it were that, it would not condition an infinite recurrence of identical cases, but a final state. *Because* the world has not reached this, mechanistic theory must be considered an imperfect and merely provisional hypothesis. (KGW VIII 14 [188], Nietzsche's emphases)

This argument, though riddled with mistakes and confusions, nevertheless makes clear Nietzsche's commitment to a fully determined course of nature, even if in places he in words denies determinism as such. (I here put aside the issue of "mechanism" for discussion in connection with the theory of the will to power.) But, one might ask, what other than an assumption of a thorough, strict causal determinism would make anything like this argument for eternal return even initially plausible? I think that appropriate answer is: nothing other than this assumption. But then how shall we accommodate Nietzsche's denial of determinism, not to mention the official topic of this chapter, causality itself, as well as laws of nature?

Let us remind ourselves that, in general and when he is not in his "all-is-chaos" frame of mind, Nietzsche affirms that nature has regularity, recurrence, calculability, predictability, and inalterability while, often in the same context, denying that it has causality, lawfulness, and a deterministic structure. As for necessity: it sometimes is placed with what is affirmed, sometimes with what is denied. What we must now understand is that, on one major contemporary understanding of causation and lawfulness, Nietzsche's view of reality is a deterministic one--of the full causation, by way of laws of nature, of everything that happens. It is also, I believe, the correct ontology of causation and lawfulness.

That theory is, probably needless to say, one that derives from the thought of David Hume. But, at least as I shall formulate it, it is not exactly his view. More importantly, and as I stressed above, it is not, as both Hume and Nietzsche are prone to say, a view that denies that there is causation and lawfulness, but instead a particular ontology of those aspects of reality.

Let us start with causation. On the view in question, and to take the simplest case: for two events to be *causally* connected just is for them to be *lawfully* related. It is not required on this view, as some critics have supposed, that if, in a particular case, an event of kind A causes an event of kind B, there be a simple, strict law that whenever an event of kind A occurs, it be followed by an event of kind B. All that is required is that there be some law that mentions events of kind A in its antecedent (assuming the law is formulated in the familiar "if-then" way), possibly among events of other kinds, such as "If A and C and D, then B." We say, for example, in the case of some particular person, that his smoking cigarettes over many years caused his lung cancer. And so it probably did, not because there is a law that anyone who smokes cigarettes over many years gets lung cancer, but because there is some law of nature that connects smoking to lung cancer. So, to repeat, causation requires–indeed just is– lawful connection, but not necessarily invariable connection.

But, as we speak, not all cases of lawful connection, not even all cases of earlier to later events, are ones of causal connection. That is why I like to say sometimes that causation is lawfulness plus *context*. What this means is again best explained by example: A car with faulty but not inoperable brakes being driven by a drunk driver on an icy road runs off the road at a curve in the road even though the driver applies the brakes, and kills a cow. Furthermore, it is a fact, determinable or not, that if any of those conditions–bad brakes, drunk driver, icy road–had not obtained, the car would not have run off the road. Which condition is the cause of the accident? Depending on the *context*–concern with good automobiles, legal responsibility, construction of statistics of accidents in bad weather–each may be said to be, not just a causal factor, but even *the* cause of the accident.

Even though there are many other ways in which context determines whether or not we *say* that some event or condition was *a* or *the* cause of some other event or condition, the idea is clear. But in all such cases, now to repeat, lawful connections are involved, and that is the crucial matter. And because context is, ontologically speaking, nothing, we may say again that causation just is lawful connection. The negative claim is that there is no entity–the "causal connection" or a "necessary connection"–in the particular case, as both Hume and Nietzsche knew and emphasized.

Both Hume and Nietzsche also were highly interested in the psychological side of our ascriptions of causation in the absence of any observable entity in the particular causal situation but, in my opinion, in the wrong way. The most interesting psychological fact, which, to my knowledge, neither of them dealt with, is that our knowledge of certain causal connections is too quick and immediate to ascribe to mere generalization from particular cases. This is not the place to discuss this phenomenon in detail; with others, I suggest that we are, as an evolutionary perspective would strongly imply anyway, "pre-programmed" to regard certain kinds of situation as causal ones, for survival very much requires our being able to do so from the moment we are born. Surely it is not a matter of perception of a further entity between the cause and the effect.

But if causation just is, in the relevant sense, lawful connection, that leaves the much more interesting and difficult question of what, in nature itself, lawful connection is. What is the ontology of lawfulness? Nietzsche, we know and saw, believes that our conception of lawfulness, like causation itself, somehow involves willing or intention; and I have already had my say on that. It is unfortunate that, at least in all major European languages, the word 'law' and its relatives cover both--on the one hand (1) the normative notion obviously involved in the laws of a government or state or other institutions designed to regulate behavior as well as the prescriptions said to be "handed down" by this or that deity and, finally, so-called "natural laws" of rights and obligations said somehow to be woven into the fabric of nature itself (or perhaps human nature); and, on the other hand (2) the kinds of laws that we are here discussing–what scientists try to discover about how the universe actually "ticks", independent of all prescriptions, desires, fears, and values. But we should be able, even if Nietzsche and so many others were and are not, clearly to distinguish these very different things, even granted that the language of the former sometimes carries over into that of the latter, as when we say that nature is "governed" by (scientific) laws.

But even if we empty the notion of a scientific law of all normative and intentional content, we are still left with the question of what such a law *is*, especially granted that it, like causation itself, is not something that can be simply observed. The ontology of laws of nature, especially in distinguishing them from so-called "accidental" generalities, is very difficult. Once again, there seems to be nothing there; yet the distinction between those universal propositions that warrant (true) counterfactual conditionals and those that do not is there, reflecting a difference in nature itself. One can say, not entirely idly, that laws have to do with the natures of the properties involved while accidental generalities do not (except negatively), or that laws have to do with necessary connections between and among properties as exemplified by particular things while accidental generalities do not. But that is more to restate the question than to answer it. In any case, the necessity involved is not logical necessity but only lawful or, if one likes, causal necessity.

Nor can one accept the simple solution that would put empirical laws in the same category of truths as those directly about properties, such as 'Red is darker than pink.' This truth about red and pink supports the derived truth that red things are darker than pink things. And things that are water and heated to 212° F boil as a matter of lawful necessity; but the properties of being water and being 212° F do not boil. Thus lawful truths are of quite a different kind from those about properties.

Although we have not arrived at a definite theory as to the ontology of lawfulness, we may now return to Nietzsche. For enough has been said to suggest the likelihood that lawfulness is nothing more than the regularity, calculability, and inalterability that he willingly ascribes to nature. About necessity, Nietzsche is, as we know, somewhat more cautious, if that is the right word, apparently fearing at certain times that thinking of the course of nature as being one of necessity is thinking of it teleologically. Yet, as we also saw, he sometimes also does ascribe necessity also to nature itself.

As for determinism, we may say that, despite his verbal rejection of it here and there, Nietzsche is a determinist. At the human level, this means a rejection of free will as it is often, and also by Nietzsche, conceived; that is, as a lack of full causation of human choices. For *all* is "regular", all is (in principle) "calculable," and it is wholly contrary to Nietzsche's deepest impulses to suppose that human beings somehow have escaped, even in part, from the natural order of things. We are products of nature only, and Nietzsche regards it as not only one of the errors but also one of the immoralities of religion that it teaches that we are not only in the obvious biological and other related ways different from other animals and species, but different in a much more profound, even ontological, way–that we are the special products of the gods, and more like them in fundamental ways than other organisms. It is one of his projects, he says, to "read" us back into nature, getting rid of religious notions of guilt, sin, and free will. A final quote for this chapter, this time from *The Antichrist*, goes to this point as well as his commitment to scientific understanding, and even "mechanistic explanation", in general:

> We no longer derive man from "the spirit" or "the deity"; we have placed him back among the animals. . . . On the other hand we oppose the vanity that would raise its head again here too–as if man had been the great hidden purpose of the evolution of the animals. . . .
> As regards the animals, Descartes was the first to have dared, with admirable boldness, to understand the animal as *machina*: the whole of our physiology endeavors to prove this claim. And we are consistent enough not to except man, as Descartes still did: our knowledge of man today goes just as far as we understand him mechanistically. Formerly man was give a "free will" as his dowry from a higher order: today we have taken his will away altogether, in the sense that we no longer admit the will as a faculty. (A 14)

At the cosmic level, we saw that his doctrine of eternal return requires a deterministic universe. Whether or not he really believed that very dubious doctrine doesn't really matter; he thought it was possible in any case in the sense that the universe was in its fundamental aspects such that recurrence was not impossible. But independent of his commitment to the doctrine, it is clear that he believed the universe to be without beginning or end, and to be "inalterable" in what I think is the sense of being such that no one and nothing can change its course from what it would have been by somehow "breaking" its laws. And we know how Nietzsche scoffed at the idea of miracles in exactly that sense.

So where does all of this leave us on Nietzsche on causation? I have, effectively, already stated my answer. Nietzsche recognizes the world to be such that, as causation and lawfulness are widely and (in my view) correctly analyzed ontologically, it is a world of causation and lawfulness. His fuss, as I like to call it, about both of these notions has worthy motivation insofar as it is directed against, on the one hand, anthropological and theological notions of intention and willing, and, on the other hand, ontological notions of a causal entity as such in the particular case being analytically involved in these notions. And while, in much of his discourse about causation and, to a much lesser extent, lawfulness in his everyday talk about ordinary causal situations, Nietzsche takes these notions entirely for granted, as he and anyone well should, he doesn't seem to realize that they can be given ontological treatment that retains their perfectly respectable status when regarded philosophically, even though he himself has provided the necessary elements for that treatment.

But there are two residues, as it were. One we have already discussed–his denial of "things" and its alleged consequence that no there is therefore not sufficient orderliness in the world for the application of notion such as causation. The other, which I have hardly mentioned so far, is that of the will to power, which is sometimes claimed by Nietzsche to be the only entity of causal efficacy.

So let us turn, in a final chapter, to Nietzsche's theory of the will to power.

THE WILL TO POWER

Looked at from a certain "perspective" (which is probably Nietzsche's own), it is his theory of the will to power at the cosmological level that is of greatest importance to his views of the nature of reality. But much, perhaps most, of his discussion is of the will to power in human beings, and I shall take some initial note of that; and, to a lesser extent in the domain of organic things generally. While there are some important passages to ponder in other works, especially *Thus Spake Zarathustra*, most of Nietzsche's writing on the subject occurs in *The Will to Power*. And, like much in that book, much of that discussion has a somewhat tentative character, as if Nietzsche was still trying to arrive at a satisfactory (to him) account of the will to power. This applies especially to what I call his "cosmological" theory, that is, the idea of the will to power as applying to everything–inorganic matter, organisms in general, and human beings in particular. Still, in an essay on Nietzsche's ontology, it is necessary and important to say something about this aspect of how, in fundamental ways, reality is or at least may be, according to Nietzsche.

As with causation, so with will: Nietzsche sometimes sees it everywhere, sometimes nowhere. In the chapter on mind, we saw, and I emphasized, his denial of the efficacy of will. But I have also said somewhere that Nietzsche seems often, in the case of human beings, to confuse the ordinary will, which operates or at least appears in the particular case, with the will to power. Or, more charitably and perhaps more accurately said, he does not always make clear to the reader, when it would be relevant and helpful, the distinction anyone should make between the ordinary, more or less conscious, everyday will on the one hand, and, on the other hand, the basic impulse that, on his view, underlies human behavior in general. By my account, Nietzsche thinks little of the ordinary human will in the sense not only that it is not causally efficacious but also that its study tells us little if anything about what is fundamentally going on in human beings.

There is a long tradition, before and after and including Nietzsche, that more or less takes for granted that there is a single, basic impulse underlying all human behavior. According to this or that particular theory, this impulse will be said to be peculiar to human beings, or to a certain subset of kinds of organisms including human beings, to all kinds of organisms, or–as in Nietzsche's case–to everything whatsoever. Yet, even in Nietzsche's case the form that it takes in human beings is so different, though perhaps only in its complexity, that he could consistently have asserted it only of human beings. In any case, as I said above, Nietzsche devotes much of his discussion of the will to power as it appears in humans. And although, as I indicated above, this is not really germane to my main topic of Nietzsche's ontology, I shall briefly compare his theory, as he himself does in part, to other single-impulse theories, beginning by quoting one of my favorite passages in Nietzsche, which appears in one of my least favorite works, *Thus Spake Zarathustra*:

> And life itself confided this secret to me: "Behold," it said, "I am *that which must always overcome itself.* Indeed, you call it a will to procreate or a drive to an end, to something higher, farther, more manifold: but all this is one, and one secret.
> "Rather would I perish that forswear this; and verily, where there is perishing and a falling of leaves, behold, there life sacrifices itself–for power. That I must be struggle and a becoming and an end and an opposition to ends–alas, whoever guesses what is my will should also guess on what *crooked* paths it must proceed.
> "Whatever I create and however much I love it–soon I must oppose it and my love; thus my will wills it. And you too, lover of knowledge, are only a path and footprint of my will; verily, my will to power walks also on the heels of your will to truth.
> "Indeed, the truth was not him by him who shot at it with the word of the 'will to existence': that will does not exist. For, what does not exist cannot will; but what is in existence, how could that still want existence? Only where there is life is there also will: not will to life but–thus I teach you–will to power.
> "There is much that life esteems more highly than life itself, but out of the esteeming itself speaks the will to power." (Z II "On Self-Overcoming")

If we combine what is said in this passage with Nietzsche's extensive criticism elsewhere of the theory that the desire for pleasure is the basic human impulse, we can list the following as being what humans fundamentally desire or pursue, according to the theories he opposes, with my indication for each of a philosopher who might be considered the, or at least a, main proponent:

being (will to existence)	Jean-Paul Sartre
sexual pleasure (will to procreate)	Sigmund Freud

pleasure in general (will to pleasure)	John Stuart Mill
knowledge (will to truth)	Plato
higher goal (will to an end)	Thomas Aquinas

Of course, for Sartre it is what he calls the "desire to be God," the contradictory combination of contingent and necessary being, that is our fundamental impulse, as expressed in each of our unique "original projects"; so, obviously, is not quite what Nietzsche had in mind. But I am not interested in pursuing the matter of what, if anything, is the fundamental human impulse, except to observe (1) that as Freud explicitly does, and as any single-impulse theorist should do, Nietzsche also accepts the task of explaining (but not in the passage above) how behaviors that seem to be exceptions or even falsifying instances of the theory are to be accommodated to the theory, and (2) that what I have been calling "impulses" to behavior, whether fundamental or not, and whether single or multiple, are to be treated ontologically as dispositions and thus as physiological configurations subject to certain laws of nature.

As for the will to power with respect to life in general, we need not tarry, even though, in at least three places--*Beyond Good and Evil* 259, *The Gay Science* 349, and *The Will to Power* 254--Nietzsche characterizes the will to power simply as the will to life, even seeming to define 'life' that way in the last of these passages:

> But *what is life?* Here we need a new, more definite formulation of the concept "life." My formula for it is: Life is will to power. (KGW VIII 2 [190], Nietzsche's emphases)

But the context of the discussion in all three of these passages makes clear that Nietzsche intends neither to exclude the non-living part of the universe from the will to power nor, more radically, to regard all there is as living. What is more interesting about Nietzsche's notion of the will to power in connection with life is his critique of Darwinism–not of evolution itself, but of natural selection and "survival of the fittest" as its mechanism. But, interesting as it is, this matter is not one of ontology.

With that, I turn to the main topic–the will to power as the basic, and perhaps the only, force in everything.

The most important thing to be said at the outset is that, despite Nietzsche's occasional attempts to enlist the notion of will in defense of his theory (as in the oft-quoted entry 36 of *Beyond Good and Evil*, of which more later), it is the notion of power and not of will that is the more important notion (as Richard Schacht also affirms in his extended and extremely valuable discussion of the will to power in his 1983, 212-234). For there is no intention, not even in the extended sense in which unconscious mental states may be said to be intentional, in the notion when applied to nature at large. For there is no consciousness, nothing mental, at all in most of nature. There is no goal, no end, no purpose but only a force or power that operates in a certain way. It would have been far better for what he means had Nietzsche found another expression, one that more accurately captures the nature of the power involved without suggesting that it is "willed". (And, not incidentally, it would have made it more difficult for his sister and the National Socialists plausibly to enlist him as a progenitor of their nefarious causes.) I cannot think of any expression, however, that rolls off the tongue and has the rhetorical strength of 'the will to power' or, more importantly, '*der Wille zur Macht*' for what Nietzsche is talking about. But 'universal expansive force' would certainly have been more nearly precise in description.

What happened, historically speaking, or so I opine, is that Nietzsche first thought of the will to power primarily, maybe even exclusively, with respect to human beings, as the passage quoted above from *Thus Spake Zarathustra* might be taken to illustrate. And in that context, the notion of will, though perhaps only in the extended sense, is applicable. But when he came to see the idea of power as having universal application–not only to humans or even only to life, but to everything living and non-living–he was stuck with the notion of will there too, even though it really has no sense at all, except perhaps in the doubly extended sense in which various processes and configurations of nature can sometimes seem to be *as if* they were willed. Naturally, the ghost of Arthur Schopenhauer is also hovering in the background of Nietzsche's terminology and theory, not to mention numerous other thinkers of the time (whom we know Nietzsche read) who were pursuing questions about force, energy, matter, and the like, on the borderline between empirical science and philosophy, much as Descartes and Leibniz and others had done two hundred years earlier. It might be said that Nietzsche failed to absorb the lesson that in such matters, as in conflicts with religion, empirical science always "wins" in the long run.

But I shall proceed, largely ignoring both the historical and systematic connections of Nietzsche's theory to Schopenhauer's or anyone else's

So the question becomes: what is the nature of this universal force that Nietzsche believes to exist, and how, in a general way, does it operate?

It is not easy to get into the question of the nature of the will to power, as Nietzsche conceives it, for, as indicated above, most of what he says on the matter is in his notes included in *The Will to Power*, which are, by their nature, tentative and self-directed. Further, and more important, they are vague, ambiguous, and internally inconsistent, at least on the surface. But one must jump in somewhere, trying to makes some kind of overall sense of it. This has already been done in one way by Schacht, as also indicated above, and of course many others have also had their say. But I propose to go about the matter somewhat differently, perhaps putting more emphasis on the weaknesses of the theory.

Let us begin with Nietzsche's apparent conception of his theory as an addition and even consummation of "mechanistic" theory, which is usually, and here too though more mildly than usual, one of his *bêtes noires*. This note (WP 619) of summer 1885 reads:

> The victorious concept "force," by means of which our physicists have created God and the world, still needs to be completed: an inner will must be ascribed to it, which I designate as "will to power," i.e., as an insatiable desire to manifest power; or as the employment and exercise of power, as a creative drive, etc. Physicists cannot eradicate "action at a distance" from their principles; nor can they eradicate a repellent force (or an attracting one). There is nothing for it: one is obliged to understand all motion, all "appearances," all "laws," only as symptoms of an inner event and to employ man as an analogy to this end. In the case of an animal, it is possible to trace all its drives to the will to power; likewise all the functions of organic life to this one source. (KGW VII 36 [31])

(The "mechanistic" theory is described in the preceding entry, accused of having a "hole" that prevents it from really explaining what it purports to explain.) Putting aside his characterization of this power as a "desire", which in any case is softened by his writing of man as an "analogy" in its understanding, we find Nietzsche suggesting that adding the will to power to what the physicists already have will enable the explanation of the otherwise mysterious fact of action at a distance, something physicists and philosophers had worried about at least since the publication of Isaac

Newton's *Principia Mathematica.* Perhaps it is as if someone described the behavior of, say, a computer without mentioning the power source, the electricity that keeps it running. Or, at a very different level, one might be reminded of the theory, Descartes's among others', that without God's constant "sustaining" embrace of what he created, the universe would just stop "running", either cease existing or cease changing. At the same time, we are to understand this power as an "inner event," that is, not as something merely added to "things" from without, as it were, but as inherent in them as "things" or whatever "they" are. In this respect, one is reminded of Leibniz and his insistence that substances, even if created, have an inherent capacity for change, one that is not dependent on God's "sustaining" them (although, of course, God has the power to cause them to cease to exist).

At the same time, I think one should resist Arthur Danto's suggestion in his *Nietzsche as Philosopher,* 215, that the will to power be thought of as significantly similar to substances, as much of the tradition conceived them. To be sure, in some sense the will to power "underlies" everything there is and, at least in us and perhaps other organisms, secondary impulses might be thought of as "modifications" of the fundamental impulse of the will to power. But, not to mention the fact that Nietzsche explicitly rejects any idea of substance in his conception of reality (admittedly not a decisive fact), there is nothing that, at least by intention, corresponds to that fundamental feature of individual substances; namely, that of having a nature or essence that marks its commonality with others of its kind but, more important here, distinguishes it, qualitatively, from other substances. Furthermore, but mysteriously, Nietzsche tells us that the will to power is not a "being," a matter to which I shall return.

At a certain level, perhaps the basic one, the will to power is to be understood as consisting of "quanta" of power. And although, at least in one passage (which I shall quote further on) he himself refers to such a quantum as an atom, Nietzsche in general scoffs at the belief that there are atoms, regarding them as the physicist's extension of the traditional notion of substance. At the same time, Nietzsche is quite aware of the fundamental reason that the physicist "posits" a realm of invisible entities, which is that of providing satisfactory explanations of phenomena in the realm of visible entities (sight being not the only, but the most important, sense for the matter at hand). Indeed, Nietzsche says as much in a note dated 1883-

1888 (WP 624), while at the same time challenging the reality of the posited entities–atoms–and the value of what has been achieved:

> *Against* the physical *atom*.— To comprehend the world, we have to be able to calculate it; to be able to calculate it, we have to have constant causes; because we find no such constant causes in actuality, we invent them for ourselves–the atoms. This is the origin of atomism.
> The calculability of the world, the expressibility of all events in formulae–is this really "comprehension"? How much of a piece of music has been understood when that in it which is calculable and can be reduced to formulas has be reckoned up?—And "constant causes," things, substances, something "unconditioned"; *invented*–what has one achieved? (KGW VIII 7 [56], Nietzsche's emphases)

Here we have a view that looks much like instrumentalism in contemporary philosophy of science (putting aside the romantic fuss about understanding music, which, I would agree, has a point). But it is important to notice that Nietzsche is rejecting the *physical* atom and not the possibility that, in some sense, there is a smallest kind of entity. (Let us remember that Nietzsche is writing at a time before the word 'atom' as used by physicists got "locked in" at a certain level, so that we now speak of the *constituents* of atoms, something that would have been simply contradictory at his time.) Thus we may understand that, for Nietzsche, there are some invisible, indivisible entities of some sort, which are necessary to explain features of the visible world, especially and crucially motion, but which are not physical atoms. But nor, of course, are they mental atoms. They are instead, it would seem, quanta not of matter or mind but of *energy*. The distinction between matter and energy, and how it is treated in contemporary physics, need not concern us except to the extent of noting that Nietzsche and his contemporaries regarded it as being of great importance, and not just in physics narrowly conceived. For, if I am not mistaken, it represents for those at the time the old distinction of philosophers between the inherently passive and the inherently active. For these thinkers, if matter were the ultimate reality, there would be no change, no "becoming", no motion. So, it is not the ultimate reality. For some thinkers, this would be the place to invoke minds of some kind, natural or, more likely, supernatural. But for the modernist thinkers of the nineteenth century, this was no longer a believable alternative. Instead, one had the possibility that energy was the ultimate reality, with its comfortable implication that change and motion were not just natural but inevitable. And this, I submit, is the framework in which we may understand Nietzsche's notion of the will to power as consisting of "dynamic quanta". Some of these suggestions, as well as other now familiar themes, are sounded in what is, arguably, the single most important passage in Nietzsche for understanding his theory of the will to power at the cosmic level, a note dated March-June 1888 (WP 634), the last year, we may again emphasize, of his active life. It is a long entry, but probably worth quoting in full:

> *Critique of the mechanistic theory.*— Let us here dismiss the two popular concepts "necessity" and "law": the former introduces a false constraint into the world, the latter a false freedom. "Things" do not behave regularly, according to a *rule*: there are no things (—they are fictions invented by us); they behave just as little under the constraint of necessity. There is no obedience here: for that something is as it is, as strong or as weak, is not the consequence of an obedience to a rule or a compulsion—
> The degree of resistance and the degree of superior power—this is the question in every event: if, for our day-to-day calculations, we know how to express this in formulas and "laws," so much the better for us! But we have not introduced any "morality" into the world by the fiction that it is obedient—.
> There is no law: every power draws its ultimate consequence at every moment. Calculability exists precisely because things are unable to be other than they are.
> A quantum of power is designated by the effect it produces and that which it resists. The adiaphorous state is missing, though it is thinkable. It is essentially a will to violate and to defend oneself against violation. Not self-preservation: every atom affects the whole of being—it is thought away if one thinks away this radiation of power-will. That is why I call it a quantum of "will to power"; it expresses the characteristic that it cannot be thought out of the mechanistic order without thinking away this order itself.
> A translation of this world of effect into a visible world–a world for the eyes–is the conception "motion." This always carries the idea that *something* is moved–this always supposes, whether as the fiction of a little clump of atom or even as the abstraction of this, the dynamic atom, a thing that produces effects–i.e., we have not got away from the habit into which our senses and language seduce us. Subject, object, a doer added to the doing, the doing separated from that which it does: let us not forget that this is mere semeiotics and nothing real. Mechanistic theory as a theory of motion is already a translation into the sense language of man. (KGW VIII 14 [79], Nietzsche's emphases)

Thus, as a quantum (or even "atom") of energy, this basic constituent of the will to power possesses that fundamental feature of the will to power considered as a whole; namely, the inherent capacity to expand against, or "violate," that which is nearby and thus to affect everything there is. And as such, it is the cause of motion and change. But this is not, apparently, a "war of all against all"; this propensity to "violation" is tempered by the fact of the encountering other such entities, as Nietzsche tells us in a note of the same date as that immediately above (WP 636):

> My idea is that every specific body strives to become master over all space and to extend its force (—its will to power:) and to thrust back all that resists its extension. But it continually encounters similar efforts on the part of other bodies and ends by coming to an arrangement ("union") with those of them that are sufficiently related to it: thus they conspire together for power. And the process goes on— (KGW VIII 14 [186])

Thus, the ultimate reality (or so it seems, pending a further twist in the dialectic to come) for Nietzsche consists of these "dynamic quanta"–ultimate in the analytic sense of being the simplest entities out of which everything else is constituted or from which in some fashion derived. In that important sense, too, the will to power is the fundamental feature of Nietzsche's ontology, assuming, as I have, that we may treat his ontology as a whole, from both his writings intended for publication and his notes, that is, including, most importantly, the notes published as *The Will to Power*. For this assumption, I have made no serious argument, being more interested in what ontology we can find, formulate, and to some extent develop from what Nietzsche wrote than in what otherwise Nietzsche might be thought to have believed. I have mildly chastised Nietzsche and others, especially the "postmodernists," for putting forth theories that they could not possibly believe, or act as if they believed (else, in some cases, they would not be here to put them forward); but the point here is more, in conformity with the task of what Gustav Bergmann called the "structural historian,' to try to formulate accounts of what one believes the thinker in question was, however vaguely and sometimes confusedly, trying to get at, and not, necessarily, what was actually in his mind as he wrote. And this is what I have attempted to do throughout, but especially with respect to the theory of the will to power, which is why I stress it here.

But we are not finished with the theory. For I have promised to say something about two passages, both of which I and some others find in need of explication. The first is the well-known passage from *Beyond Good and Evil,* which, though long, needs to be quoted in full, being arguably the most important statement of his theory to be found in Nietzsche's writings intended for publication, and which I have quoted before:

> Suppose nothing were "given" as real except our world of desires and passions, and we could not get down, or up, to any other "reality" besides the reality of our drives–for thinking is merely a relation of these drives to each other: is it not permitted to make the experiment and to ask the question whether this "given" would not be *sufficient* for also understanding on the basis of this kind of thing the so-called mechanistic (or "material") world? I mean, not as a deception, as "mere appearance," an "idea" (in the sense of Berkeley and Schopenhauer) but as holding the same rank of reality as our affect–as a more primitive form of the world of affects in which everything still lies contained in a powerful unity before it undergoes ramifications and developments in the organic process (and, as is only fair, becomes tenderer and weaker)–as a kind of instinctive life in which all organic functions are still synthetically intertwined along with self-regulation, assimilation, nourishment, excretion, and metabolism–as a *pre-form* of life.
>
> In the end not only is it permitted to make this experiment; the conscience of *method* demands it. Not to assume several kinds of causality until the experiment of making do with a single one has been pushed to its utmost limit (to the point of nonsense, if I may say so)--that is a moral of method which one may not shirk today--it follows "from its definition," as a mathematician would say. The question is in the end whether we really recognize the will as *efficient*, whether we believe in the causality of the will: if we do–and at bottom our faith in this is nothing less than our faith in causality itself–then we have to make the experiment of positing the causality of the will hypothetically as the only one. "Will," of course, can affect only "will'–and not "matter" (not "nerves," for example). In short, one has to risk the hypothesis whether will does not affect will wherever "effects" are recognized–and whether all mechanical occurrences are not, insofar as a force is active in them, will force, effects of will.
>
> Suppose, finally, we succeeded in explaining our entire instinctive life as the development and ramification of *one* basic form of the will–namely, of the will to power, as *my* proposition has it; suppose all organic functions could be traced back to this will to power and one could also find in it the solution to the problem of procreation and nourishment–it is *one* problem–then one would have gained the right to determine *all* efficient force univocally as–*will to power*. The world viewed from inside, the world defined and determined according to its "intelligible character"–it would be "will to power" and nothing else.—
> (BGE 36, Nietzsche's emphases)

Although, in this passage, Nietzsche clearly distinguishes the will to power in the world at large from its form in the organic and human realms (and, indeed, recognizes the prior and independent existence of the world at large from that of life), he nevertheless "models" the will to power in general on its human or at least organic expression, as a "pre-form" of life, even though he has just called it "a kind of instinctive life" with some of the attendant properties that only organisms have or can have. Perhaps we should say that here (in 1886) Nietzsche is just beginning to think seriously of the will to power on the cosmic level, generalizing, so to speak, from the human and other organic levels, and so, as yet, unable wholly to free himself from features that really pertain only to those levels in conceiving the cosmic level. Yet, curiously, once he has used the organic and human levels to conceive the cosmic level, and to argue for the exclusivity of will as causal at the level, he returns to the human level in the final paragraph to complete the story, so to speak, as if that needed to be re-argued or, at least, re-stated. And in now conceiving the world at large by its "intelligible character," Nietzsche is still bound by a conception of the will to power itself as essentially defined by its human form. From this limitation, he increasingly frees himself in his notes of *The Will to Power*, as we have just seen.

Another aspect of this limitation, as I have just called it, is the emphasis on "will" instead of "power". Earlier, I expressed my agreement with Schacht that, at least at the cosmic level and perhaps even at the organic and human levels, it is the idea of power and not that of will that is more important in understanding Nietzsche's idea of the will to power. But it must be admitted that this passage does not particularly support that approach. At the same time, I submit that Nietzsche himself, as expressed in the notes of his last two active years, came increasingly to reverse the earlier emphasis, seeing that it was power ("energy") and not will that is essential to the theory he wants to convey.

Of course, the main point of the passage is not so much to assert the ubiquity of the will to power but its status as the sole causal force. About Nietzsche on causation in general, I had my say in the last chapter. This passage, like numerous others, is one in which Nietzsche takes the existence of causation entirely for granted, as one should, but thinks of it, as have so many others, as involving force or some such entity, as one should not, or so I argued in the previous chapter. Here, though, I want to make a different point: that in giving explanations of particular occurrences of any kind, the principle of different effects/different causes is surely to be accepted, as Nietzsche himself often recognizes in practice. Purported explanations, whether that of the will to power or the will of some god or anything else, that cite some undifferentiated entity in every case, do not tell us why something happened instead of not happening, as a good explanation does. In that sense, while one might say, putting aside all other possible objections to the theory, that the will to power is the sole, efficient *force* in the world, it cannot be, thinking now of causation as any relevant variable in the explanation of some particular event, that the will to power is the sole, efficient *cause* of everything that happens. Indeed, it is not the sole, efficient cause of *anything* that happens, because, once more, it can never tell us, of any particular event, why it happened instead of not happening. Here we are obviously reminded of Nietzsche's own distinction in *The Gay Science* between "the cause of acting" and "the cause of acting in a particular way" (GS, 360).

The other passage that needs commentary is a note dated March-June 1888 (WP 635), in which Nietzsche seems to be giving the will to power a very mysterious ontological status. Having listed certain things as merely "phenomenal" in the sense of being projections of the mind on the world, he continues:

> If we eliminate these additions, no things remain but only dynamic quanta, in a relation of tension to all other dynamic quanta: their essence lies in their relation to all other quanta, in their "effect" upon the same. The will to power not a being, not a becoming, but a *pathos*—the most elemental fact from which becoming and effecting first emerge— (KGW VIII 14 [79], Nietzsche's emphasis)

Walter Kaufmann, in a footnote to this passage (of which he is the translator) invites us to compare this and surrounding passages with "[Alfred North] Whitehead's philosophy of occasions and events." If what he means by this is that both Nietzsche and Whitehead seem to be suggesting an ontology in which relations are, in some important sense, more fundamental than their relata, I agree. I also believe that this is a not a fully intelligible thesis or, more charitably put, not a defensible thesis. But let us pursue the idea nevertheless.

Nietzsche's use of the word 'pathos' in the passage is, I take it, a metaphor that invites us to regard the will to power as not merely the tendency to "expand" at the possible expense of other things but, perhaps equally, as what these days would be called a "reaching out" to other things, *as if* in compassion or sympathy. And this "reaching out" is ontologically prior to that which "reaches out" and that which is "reached out" to. Independent of the metaphor and what it is intended to convey (if I am right), there remains the ontological thesis.

One point we may recognize immediately. Until the work of Bertrand Russell, no philosopher in the Western tradition gave adequate recognition to the ontological status of relations (and most of them also not to that of properties generally). Indeed the general view had been that relations do not exist or that they are only "in" the mind or, somewhat more interestingly, can be somehow reduced to non-relational properties of things. Keeping in mind this failure to regard relations as themselves having being may help us to understand why, if Nietzsche is telling us that the will to power is really a kind of relation, it is "not a being, not a becoming" even though it has ontological priority to what has being (loosely speaking, for Nietzsche) and becoming; namely, "things." But what of the thesis of ontological priority?

In listing the ways in which substance is "prior" to its accidents, Aristotle included priority in time. Although (as I attempted to show in Addis, 1972), there may be a way to understand this without supposing that substances can and do (or did) exist without any accidents, the natural, first way to read it is as asserting just that supposition. Similarly, with Nietzsche, one seems to be asked to believe that there were first only relations and then, subsequently, their relata. That, surely, is absurd as is the supposition that substances (assuming that there are such) can exist without accidents (properties). In the case of Aristotle, I suggested that he should be taken to mean that a substance can exist prior in time to any given accident that may come to inhere in it whereas no accident (what we now sometimes call a trope) can exist prior in time to the substance in which it inheres. Somewhat similarly, we might suggest that if relations are not tropes but instead (non-Platonic) universals, then they can exist prior in time to any particular entities who would be their relata in a particular case. But, contrary to what appears to be Nietzsche's more radical thesis that the will to power, conceived as relations, can exist altogether without relata, we must say that just as a substance can exist prior to any given accident but not altogether without accidents at all, so, while a relation can exist without any given relata at a certain time, it cannot exist without any relata at all.

Moreover, if properties and relations are (non-Platonic) universals, they exist in time only insofar as they are exemplified, that is, only insofar as they enter into states of affairs consisting of both themselves and the particulars that exemplify them. I conclude that the thesis that the will to power, conceived as relations that exist prior in time to their relata is, to the extent that it is intelligible, false.

But is this really Nietzsche's view? Obviously, I have pursued the ontological analysis far beyond anything that Nietzsche did conceive, or could have conceived, given that some of these ontological possibilities were themselves conceived only years after he thought and wrote. In that sense, it is certainly not a view that Nietzsche had clearly in mind. Would he, having become familiar with later developments in analytic ontology, recognize what I have put forward as what his view amounts to, without necessarily agreeing that such a formulation shows its likely falsehood? I don't know the answer to this question, but I submit to the reader my piece of "structural history" as being the best way to understand what Nietzsche is up to, in the extended sense just adumbrated, in regarding the will to power as a *pathos*.

* * *

This study on Nietzsche's ontology began with the thesis of constant change, and continued with the topics of substances and things, minds, and causation. With that of the will to power, we have come full circle in a very simple and obvious sense: that if the will to power is, at ontological root, ubiquitous and expansive energy, then change, too, is ubiquitous and eternal in the sense of having no beginning and no end in time. In a note of summer 1885 that I could well have quoted in that chapter on constant change (WP 1062), Nietzsche affirms the impossibility of "being" in the sense of absence of change (while also, interestingly–and correctly, in my opinion–affirming the fundamentally temporal nature of the mind):

> If the world had a goal, it must have been reached. If there were for it some unintended final state, this also must have been reached. If it were in any way capable of a pausing and becoming fixed, of "being," if in the whole course of its becoming it possessed even for a moment this capability of "being," then all becoming would long since have come to an end, along with all thinking, all "spirit." The fact of "spirit" as a form of becoming proves that the world has no goal, no final state, and is incapable of being. (KGW VII 36 [15])

With that, I have largely completed this study, not being disposed to grand summaries. I will remind the reader, before I let Nietzsche have the last word, and partly because he refers to both in that passage, that in this study I have not treated of either of two aspects of his view of reality that might be regarded as ontological; namely, his claim that there are no moral facts and his theory that everything that happens recurs eternally. I have not dealt with the first because it is more a denial than an affirmation of some claimed feature of reality and not the second because it is not really ontological anyway. (For myself, I believe the view about moraltiy to be almost certainly true but the theory of eternal recurrence almost certainly false.) And I will say once more that while, admittedly, we often do come across apparent protestations to the contrary, Nietzsche (like everyone) believed in an objective reality of some kind or other, and that we can and do have some knowledge of not just the general character but also of the specific occurrences and the laws governing specific occurrences of that reality. The sober Nietzsche, not the wild Nietzsche, is the one we should take seriously or, at least, more seriously, not just as to what he really believed but also as to how things are.

Another note of summer 1885 (WP 1067), although it has to do only with the general character of the will to power, may serve as the final statement here of Nietzsche's worldview:

> And do you know what "the world" is to me? Shall I show it to you in my mirror? This world: a monster of energy, without beginning, without end; a firm, iron magnitude of force that does not grow bigger or smaller, that does not expend itself but only transforms itself; as a whole, of unalterable size, a household without expenses or losses, but likewise without increase or income; enclosed by "nothingness" as by a boundary; not something blurry or wasted, not something endlessly extended, but set in a definite space as a definite force, and not a space that might be "empty" here or there, but rather as force throughout, as a play of forces and waves of forces, at the same time one and many, increasing here and the same time decreasing there; a sea of forces flowing and rushing together, eternally changing, eternally flooding back, with tremendous years of recurrence, with an ebb and a flood of its forms; out of the simplest forms striving toward the most complex, out of the stillest, most rigid, coldest forms toward the hottest, most turbulent, most self-contradictory, and then again returning home to the simple out of this abundance, out of the play of contradictions back to the joy of concord, still affirming itself in this uniformity of its courses and its years, blessing itself as that which must return eternally, as a becoming that knows no satiety, no disgust, no weariness: this my *Dionysian* world of the

eternally self-creating, the eternally self-destroying, this mystery world of the twofold voluptuous delight, my "beyond good and evil," without goal, unless the joy of the circle is itself a goal; without will, unless a ring feels good will toward itself–do you want a *name* for this world? A *solution* for all its riddles? A *light* for you, too, you best-concealed, strongest, most intrepid, most midnightly men?— *This world is the will to power—and nothing besides!* And you yourselves are also this will to power—and nothing besides! (KGW VII 38 [12], Nietzsche's emphases)

BIBLIOGRAPHY

Addis, Laird. 1972. "Aristotle and the Independence of Substances." *Philosophy and Phenomenological Research* 33: 107-111.

_____. 1975. *The Logic of Society: A Philosophical Study*. Minneapolis: University of Minnesota Press.

_____. 1981. "Dispositions, Explanation, and Behavior." *Inquiry* 24: 205-227.

_____. 1984. "Parallelism, Interactionism, and Causation." in *Causation and Causal Theories*, edited by Peter French, Theodore Uehling, and Howard Wettstein. Minneapolis: University of Minnesota Press, 329-344.

_____. 1989. *Natural Signs: A Theory of Intentionality*. Philadelphia: Temple University Press.

Aristotle. 1941. *Metaphysics*. (translated by W. D. Ross) in *The Basic Works of Aristotle*, edited by Richard McKeon. New York: Random House.

Audi, Robert (ed.). 1999. *The Cambridge Dictionary of Philosophy* (2nd edition). Cambridge: Cambridge University Press.

Bergmann, Gustav. 1959a. "Some Reflections on Time." in his *Meaning and Existence*. Madison: The University of Wisconsin Press, 225-263.

_____. 1959b. "The Revolt Against Logical Atomism." in his *Meaning and Existence*. Madison: The University of Wisconsin Press, 39-72.

_____. 1964. "Realistic Postscript." in his *Logic and Reality*. Madison: The University of Wisconsin Press, 302-340.

Casullo, Albert. 1988. "A Fourth Version of the Bundle Theory." *Philosophical Studies* 54: 125-139.

Clark, Maudemarie. 1990. *Nietzsche on Truth and Philosophy*. Cambridge: Cambridge University Press.

Danto, Arthur. 1965. *Nietzsche as Philosopher*. New York: Columbia University Press.

Davidson, Donald. 1970. "Mental Events." in *Experience and Theory*, edited by Lawrence Foster and J. W. Swanson. Amherst: University of Massachusetts Press, 79-101.

Hales, Steven D. and Welshon, Rex. 2000. *Nietzsche's Perspectivism*. Urbana: University of Illinois Press.

Kaufmann, Walter. 1954. *The Portable Nietzsche*. New York: Vintage Books.

Kitcher, Philip and Schacht, Richard. 2004. *Finding an Ending: Reflections on Wagner's Ring*. New York: Oxford University Press.

Kuhn, Thomas. 1962. *The Structure of Scientific Revolutions*. Chicago: The University of Chicago Press.

Leiter, Brian. 2002. *Nietzsche on Morality*. London: Routledge.

Mannheim, Karl. 1968. *Ideology and Utopia*. (translated by Louis Wirth and Edward Shils) New York: Harcourt, Brace, and World.

Poellner, Peter. 1995. *Nietzsche and Metaphysics*. Oxford: Clarendon Press.

Richardson, John. 1996. *Nietzsche's System*. Oxford: Oxford University Press.

Rorty, Richard. 1979. *Philosophy and the Mirror of Nature*. Princeton: Princeton University Press.

Schacht, Richard. 1983. *Nietzsche*. London: Routledge.

_____. 1995. *Making Sense of Nietzsche*. Urbana: University of Illinois Press.

_____. 2000. "Nietzschean Cognitivism." *Nietzsche Studien*, 29:12-40.

_____. 2011. "Nietzsche's Anti-Scientistic Naturalism." in *Nietzsches Wissenschaftsphilosophie*, edited by Helmut Heit, Günter Abel, and Marco Brusotti. Berlin, New York: de Gruyter, 161-186.

Sellars, Wilfrid. 1963. "Empiricism and the Philosophy of Mind." in his *Science, Perception, and Reality*. London: Routledge and Kegan Paul, 127-196.

Thucydides. 1954. *History of the Peloponnesian War*. (translated by Rex Warner) London: Penguin Books.

Van Cleve, James. 1985. "Three Versions of the Bundle Theory." *Philosophical Studies* 47: 95-107.

Vattimo, Gianni. 2006. *Dialogue with Nietzsche.* (translated by William McCuaig) New York: Columbia University Press.

Veatch, Henry. 1974. "To Gustav Bergmann: A Humble Petition and Advice." in *The Ontological Turn: Studies in the Philosophy of Gustav Bergmann*, edited by M. S. Gram and E. D. Klemke. Iowa City: University of Iowa Press, 65-85.

Welshon, Robert C. 1999. "Perspectivist Ontology and *de re* Knowledge." in *Nietzsche, Epistemology, and Philosophy of Science*, edited by Babette E. Babich. Dordrecht: Kluwer Academic Publishers, 39-46.

Wittgenstein, Ludwig. 1953. *Philosophical Investigations*. (translated by G. E. M. Anscombe) Oxford: Basil Blackwell.

Name Index

Addis, Laird, 10, 11, 26, 29, 30, 35, 43, 46, 71, 87, 94, 131

Aquinas, Thomas, 121

Aristotle, 1, 14, 43, 82, 111, 131

Audi, Robert, 2

Ayer, A. J., 53

Bergmann, Gustav, 1, 2, 5, 41, 52, 127

Berkeley, George, 52, 53, 78, 80, 86, 111

Brentano, Franz, 1

Casullo, Albert, 60

Clark, Maudmarie, 5, 9

Cornaro, Luigi, 104

Cratylus of Athens, 30

Danto, Arthur, 124

Darwin, Charles, 82, 121

Davidson, Donald, 98

Descartes, René, 41, 42, 44, 46, 77, 82, 89, 117, 122, 124

Dilthey, Wilhelm, 11

Freud, Sigmund, 88, 89, 91, 92, 120, 121

Galilei, Galileo, 44

Hales, Steven, 3-4, 5, 56-61
Hegel, Georg, 11, 80
Heraclitus, 30-31, 38-39
Hume, David, 52, 76, 83, 101-102, 114, 115

Kant, Immanuel, 27, 52, 53, 58, 59, 80
Kaufmann, Walter, 17, 77, 130
Kitcher, Philip, 29
Kuhn, Thomas, 11-12

Leibniz, Gottfried, 1, 80, 88-89, 122, 124
Leiter, Brian, 28-30
Lewis, C. I., 42
Lindberg, Charles, 26

Mach, Ernst, 53
Machiavelli, Niccolo, 13
Mannheim, Karl, 11, 16-17, 20, 22

Marx, Karl, 11

Michelson, Albert, 12-13, 16

Mill, John Stuart, 53, 54, 121

Morley, Edward, 12-13, 16

Newton, Isaac, 44, 123-124

Overbeck, Franz, 77

Plato, 13, 14, 24, 26, 43, 52, 121

Poellner, Peter, 5, 92-93

Quine, Willard van Orman, 60

Richardson, John, 5, 33

Rorty, Richard, 76, 90

Rousseau, Jean-Jacques, 82

Russell, Bertrand, 53, 131

Sartre, Jean-Paul, 5, 106, 120, 121

Schacht, Richard, 5, 9, 12, 20, 28-30, 71, 92, 95-97, 104, 122, 123

Schopenhauer, Arthur, 74, 80, 122, 123

Sellars, Wilfrid, 75, 76, 94

Spinoza, Benedict, 42, 44, 76-77, 106, 112

Stendahl, Henri, 15

Thucydides, 13-14, 16

Van Cleve, James, 60

Vattimo, Gianni, 10

Veatch, Henry, 44

Wagner, Richard, 29

Welshon, Robert, 3-4, 5, 56-61

Whitehead, Alfred North, 130

Wittgenstein, Ludwig, 76, 94

SUBJECT INDEX

This simple index, lacking in subentries and omitting reference to some passing uses, also fails to include the very widespread notions of knowledge and of ontology as well of other, less important, notions that might have been included in a more detailed index or one for a longer book. Bold indicates the entire chapter on the subject.

Being and becoming, 24-26, 30-31, 32, 40, 52

Bundle theory, 4, 48, 50, 55, 59-67

Causation, 2, 5, 44, 74, 83, 84, 87, 88, **101-118**, 119, 125, 126, 128, 129, 130, 132

Constant change, 2, 4, **24-40**, 48, 49, 67, 132

Continuants, 42, 44-47, 66

Determinism, 30, 86, 106, 112, 113, 114, 117

Dualism, 73, 79-83, 84

Epiphenomenalism and parallelism, 73-74, 83-88, 92, 95-99, 104

Existentialism, 5, 93, 105

Idealism, 3, 13, 54, 62-67, 69, 79-83, 84, 99

Intentionality, 8, 46, 63, 93

Laws of nature, 2, 87, 106-110, 113, 114-118, 123
Logic and mathematics, 1, 3, 47, 48, 54, 65-68, 69

Materialism, 3, 79-83, 84, 86
Meaning, 8, 110-111
Method, 12, 13, 15, 17, 22
Minds, 2, 3, 9, 11, 42, 46, 65, **71-99**, 132
Morality, 3, 5, 13, 15, 17, 20, 64, 97, 103, 104, 105, 106, 126, 133

Naturalism, 3, 10, 14, 28-30

Objective reality, 3, 4, 7, 8, 9, 17, 133
Objectivity, 4, **7-23**, 64, 65, 67, 69

Particulars and particularity, 44, 45, 49-50, 54-55, 56, 60
Perspectivism, 4, 9, 16, 18, 19, 20-22, 56-61, 65, 73
Postmodernism, 3, 8, 10, 17, 55, 58-59, 127
Properties, 34-40, 42-43, 46, 48-49, 50, 51, 54, 60, 66

Relations, 130-132
Religion, 5, 13, 17, 20, 63, 85, 103, 104, 105, 108, 117, 122

Science, 2, 3, 9, 11-12, 13, 17, 28-30, 41, 44, 60, 69, 78, 82, 109, 112, 117, 122

Senses, 1, 26, 30, 31, 38-39

Simples, 2, 45, 79

Skepticism, 10-11, 73, 76, 94

Space and time, 2, 24, 56

Structural history, 5, 127, 132

Substances, 5, 31, 32, 34, 38, **41-69**, 72, 73, 75, 76-79, 83, 102, 124, 125, 131, 132

Things, 5, 32, 34, 38, **41-69**, 78, 112, 118, 131, 132

Truth, 4, **7-23**, 26, 65-68, 69, 105, 120

Unconscious, 88-95, 122

Will to power, 2, 5, 32-33, 39-40, 44, 57, 59, 78, 93, 107, 108, 118, **119-134**

www.ingramcontent.com/pod-product-compliance
Lightning Source LLC
Chambersburg PA
CBHW040741300426
44111CB00027B/3000